TRANSFORMING IT CULTURE

HOW TO USE SOCIAL INTELLIGENCE, HUMAN
FACTORS, AND COLLABORATION TO CREATE
AN IT DEPARTMENT THAT OUTPERFORMS

Frank Wander

WILEY

John Wiley & Sons, Inc.

Published by John Wiley & Sons, Inc., Hoboken, New Jersey.
Published simultaneously in Canada.

For general information on our other products and services or for technical support, please contact our Customer Care Department within the United States at (800) 762-2974, outside the United States at (317) 572-3993 or fax (317) 572-4002.

Wiley publishes in a variety of print and electronic formats and by print-on-demand. Some material included with standard print versions of this book may not be included in e-books or in print-on-demand. If this book refers to media such as a CD or DVD that is not included in the version you purchased, you may download this material at http://booksupport.wiley.com. For more information about Wiley products, visit www.wiley.com.

Library of Congress Cataloging-in-Publication Data:

Wander, Frank, 1957–
    Transforming it culture : how to use social intelligence, human factors, and collaboration to create an IT department that outperforms / Frank Wander.
      pages cm
    Includes bibliographical references and index.
    ISBN 978-1-118-43653-0 (cloth); ISBN 978-1-118-57308-2 (ebk);
    ISBN 978-1-118-57310-5 (ebk); ISBN 978-1-118-57549-9 (ebk)
      1. Information technology—Management. 2. Electronic data processing departments—Management. I. Title.
    HD30.2.W3477 2013
    004.068—dc23   2012045107

Printed in the United States of America

10 9 8 7 6 5 4 3 2 1

The greatest revolution of our generation is the discovery that human beings, by changing the inner attitudes of their minds, can change the outer aspects of their lives.

—WILLIAM JAMES

Dedicated to the Corporate Weaver: To those great and selfless leaders who unfashionably rely on sensitivity and outflowing concern to bond with their people; who peer deeply inside them with perceptive social intelligence (sogence); who understand that the social environment is their loom and their professionals are threads of experience; who weave these threads, one to another, forming a closely connected tapestry of mind and emotion, highly productive and deeply collaborative. Done skillfully, the result is pure harmony—information and productivity flow across the fibers. This is human social fabric, the material of modern productivity—the postindustrial equivalent of an assembly line. In this factory, what matters most are not the cost and quantity of thread but the quality—and whether each thread can be tightly woven into the section of the tapestry where it is needed.

This book uses the information technology (IT) profession as a lens through which we can see the importance of understanding the human factors of productivity and how to use them to unlock IT organizational effectiveness; this is how you make IT failure a rare exception, greatly increasing the success of projects, individuals, and teams; this is how you create an IT department that outperforms and companies that outcompete. Our workers are more than mere "human resources," a dehumanizing description of talent that just reinforces the notion that professionals are interchangeable parts. They aren't—and they never were! The next productivity revolution will be launched by applying human understanding to unlock the full potential of our people. At long last, we will move beyond our industrial-era management practices and rely on trust, caring, and unselfishness to liberate the productivity of our knowledge workers.

The companies that leverage human understanding to embrace their people will own the future. The need is yesterday; the time is now.

CONTENTS

FOREWORD

Frank Wander's book, *Transforming IT Culture*, is being published at a time when the role of the chief information officer (CIO) and information technology (IT) departments are being reevaluated by chief executive officers. Wander rightfully warns IT management that they have become too dependent on process-based solutions and need to rely more on the "human factors" to improve IT results. Indeed, we have become a society that believes that business problems can be solved through integrated processes, yet everything we have learned from research at Columbia University suggests that it is the human side—those "soft skills"—that are the real difference makers for success.

At Columbia, we have a master's degree program in IT executive management that has relationships with over 125 of the most successful CIOs in the industry. These CIOs mentor and coach our students in hopes that they can help them become tomorrow's IT leaders. Our program focuses more on the soft skills portion—those very things that Frank Wander emphasizes in his book: being caring, social, unlocking the potential of staff, transforming ideas into realities, establishing social networks inside your organization, to name just a few of his strategies. Wander has been a mentor in our program at Columbia and has been instrumental in helping us deliver an important message to our students: Reliance on process only will not be enough for the successful CIO of the future.

My research has rendered remarkable consistency in the ways senior CIOs defined their successes.[1] Not surprisingly, these CIO *attributes*, as I call them, comprise mostly of the human factors highlighted in Wander's book. Unfortunately, these soft skills are usually not the focus of many up-and-coming IT managers.

My new book with Wiley due to be published in early 2013, *Strategic IT: Best Practices for IT Managers and Executives*, coauthored with my colleague Lyle Yorks, divides these CIO human factor skills into two categories: personal attributes and organizational philosophy.[2]

Yorks and I define the term *personal attributes* as 11 individual traits that appear to be keys for IT leadership. Furthermore, we relate 12 organization philosophy issues that CIOs feel are critical to the way the IT organization should operate with the business.

The results of our research are clear. Most of what brings IT success relates more to the issues articulated in *Transforming IT Culture*, that is, social intelligence, human factors, and collaboration. While so many CIOs agree with this approach, few have been able to do it successfully. We still see many CIOs with a "short shelf life" in their position—only 39 months. Yet we also see that there are CIOs that have crossed that milestone and are bringing real value to their firms. Certainly, Frank Wander's book represents what this new breed of business CIOs need to do to change the ways IT is integrated into the business world.

Dr. Arthur M. Langer
Academic Director, Executive Masters of Science in
Technology Management
Columbia University
Faculties: Graduate School of Business
Graduate School of Education
School of Continuing Education

Notes

1. A. M. Langer, Information Technology and Organizational Learning: Managing Behavioral Change Through Technology and Education (New York: CRC Press, 2011).
2. A.M. Langer and L. Yorks, Strategic IT: Best Practices for IT Managers and Executives (Hoboken, NJ: John Wiley & Sons, forthcoming).

ACKNOWLEDGMENTS

Writing a book is a significant undertaking, one even bigger than I imagined when I decided to finish *Transforming IT Culture*, given that I had started this manuscript way back in 2004. Along the way, I have had encouragement from many folks who worked for me, all of whom thought a book on the human factors of productivity was more necessary than ever. I am thankful to all of them for their support.

As I look back over this journey, many, many people come to mind. Speaking with others has enriched my knowledge and led me to great books and information sources, and their probing questions sharpened my understanding. That said, a few folks need to be specifically mentioned.

Dan Roberts, president of Ouellette & Associates Consulting, Inc., has been a great help, encouraging me to finish my book and referring me to my acquisitions editor at John Wiley & Sons. He will always stand out as someone truly genuine, who is also thoughtfully focused on the human side of IT.

Dr. Arthur Langer of Columbia University, who wrote the Foreword to this book, stands out as an individual who is making a difference in so many people's lives. Aside from being a brilliant educator, he has been both a friend and mentor. Through his nonprofit, Workforce Opportunity Services, Art provides scholarships to bright, disadvantaged kids who are in danger of being left behind; he helps them get a degree in computer science and a career in IT by placing them in corporations hungry for entry-level professionals. Art understands talent and the importance of growing it. He is truly leading the way and is a great example of the power of caring.

I would also like to thank the many professionals at Wiley who provided great support, structure, and guidance as we worked together on this book. Wiley is an excellent company that has been wonderful to collaborate with, and I would never have been able to produce a book of this quality without the help and guidance of its staff. I am proud to be a member of the Wiley family.

Most important, I would like to thank my wife, Laura, and my three sons, Alex, Chris, and Kevin, who have put up with me sitting at a computer for long hours as I researched, wrote, and reviewed each chapter. They have been a great help, reviewing content, suggesting improvements, and remaining tireless cheerleaders. I am very proud of each of them and will surely engage them in my next book.

TRANSFORMING
IT CULTURE

Introduction

We fear to know the fearsome and unsavory aspects of ourselves, but we fear even more to know the godlike in ourselves.

—ABRAHAM MASLOW

Welcome to a future where professionals count and leaders have the tools and knowledge to unlock the full potential of their talent; where companies are as concerned about their human infrastructure as they are about their networks, storage, and computers; where human understanding is seen as highly productive, and human-centric practices have replaced the selfish, cold, industrial methods that now dominate traditional corporate America. That day now dawns. The pendulum of caring is starting to swing back, and its movement will produce winners and losers. How will things turn out for you?

This book will give you an awareness of the human factors of productivity, enabling you to unlock hidden pockets of personal and group effectiveness, thereby ensuring you are positioned for long-term success. Your outcome does not have to be in doubt. This is a meaningful read, and the first steps in your journey toward a higher level of performance. Enjoy it.

So, how do I know the pendulum is moving? Some things in life are just accidental. As an information technology (IT) leader, I was always very good at strategy, process, and technology, but I also cared deeply about my people and fought to create high-performing cultures where each of them really did count; they repaid the caring with on-time projects, great solutions, deep collaboration, positive social chemistry, and organizational effectiveness. The bargain was unwritten but very clear.

Because of my track record of timely delivery and innovation, I was given the opportunity to turn around departments that were struggling or deeply in trouble. Soon I was fortunate enough to lead turnarounds across companies, and it was then that a pattern emerged: The root cause of failure was the toxic behavior and practices of management itself. These behaviors and practices were not isolated to a company or even an industry—they were part of business. Serendipitously, I had come to see that caring had high productive value, and it was a blind spot. Fortunately, this blind spot has been illuminated, and the pendulum of caring is in motion, even if it isn't yet visible to you. Higher productivity leads to increased returns on human capital and competitive advantage. The companies that embrace their workers will win; the dinosaurs will fade away.

Once I understood the root cause, I was left wondering why caring is so productive. I wasn't able to explain why, so I was moved to dig deeply into academic research and write this book. *Transforming IT Culture* reveals why caring, unselfishness, and human-centric management practices are the key to unlocking knowledge worker productivity, and why increased human understanding remains an enormous opportunity for traditional corporate America and its workers.

The Passing of an Era

When breakthroughs are made, change comes quickly. Case in point: the suitcase. Putting wheels on a suitcase is such an obvious innovation, one wonders how it could have been overlooked for so long. This improvement required no complex engineering and no leading-edge materials, yet everyone missed it. Quite simply, we were trained to accept suitcases and trunks without wheels, so everyone did—for hundreds of years! But once a better alternative appeared, suitcases without wheels disappeared quickly.

Now for something equally obvious that leaders in corporate America do not yet see: the well-documented human factors of mind and emotion. These offer far more productivity potential than the practices we currently embrace. Once this breakthrough is understood, work will change very quickly. We just have to reach the tipping point.

You see, while every era is built on an explosion of understanding, every era gives something while it takes something else away. In the industrial era, we learned to mass-produce goods and held in awe the great machines that turned raw materials into finished products. Unfortunately, craftsmen, the "machines" of the prior era, were dehumanized, becoming nothing more than good hands, mere interchangeable parts, spawning a union movement that won back a measure of self-esteem and control.

Today we have transitioned into the information economy, and a new type of craftsperson has appeared: the knowledge worker. Almost unnoticed, craftspeople have returned, toiling in modern information factories, where they utilize the raw materials of a new era: concepts. By applying networks of minds and emotions, concepts are turned into reality; here deep institutional experience and advanced technical knowledge are a competitive advantage; here human understanding is a lever of productivity; here management remains largely blind to this unfolding reality.

In a stark departure with the past, a socially intelligent and unselfish leadership paradigm will fill the cold vacuum of insensitivity that is part of our industrial heritage. Our factories will buzz with the notion of socially derived productivity, and managers will focus on designing social environments that unlock human output—in addition to managing and controlling the workers. We will learn new forms of measurement that combine both art and science, so that we can peer inside these social systems and see if they are operating effectively.

Refreshingly, we have entered a time that relies on networks of people as the means of production, not machines and process (not to say they won't be very important). As this era evolves, harmony and happiness will increase, and the economic environment will become inhospitable to the cold and socially insensitive giants of the passing era. They will transform themselves or migrate to foreign environs, where an unchanged economic environment can supply their commodity labor.

Clearly, large shifts such as this happen slowly. The industrial revolution that began in the early 1700s is bleeding into the information economy that began in 1945. Like a ship traveling from the ocean to an inland waterway, we are now passing through the brackish delta, where the water transitions from cold, to cool, and then gradually becomes warm and fresh. We eagerly journey toward the warm water, where we will stop, revitalize ourselves, and relax within the security of a caring social environment that is safe and highly productive.

The U.S. economy is already far into this delta, where our past and future are bleeding together. Research-based human understanding has been building during our journey, and it is this knowledge that will propel us along the remainder of this journey. By embracing and applying what is already known, we will finally recognize the insensitive management practices of the industrial era for what they are—a human social pathology embedded within our management culture that is a legacy of the past. Patterns of behavioral transmission like this are technically classified as memes: "a cultural unit (an idea or value or pattern of behavior) that is passed from one generation to another by non-genetic means (as by imitation); memes are the cultural counterpart of genes."[1] Passively, as managers train their successors, they add a new link to corporate America's pathological chain of inheritance.

With this insight as a backdrop, we can clearly see that the root cause of our repeated failure on large, collaborative IT projects is our ignorance of the human factors of productivity. Figure I.1 juxtaposes our unemotional, cold industrial past and our future, warmed by human understanding.

A New Era Brings a New Focus

In this new era, it is clear that social intelligence, trust, and unselfishness are indispensable management tools that enable a leader to energize a human web and make it highly productive. Executives who can do this will rise in

Figure I.1   Two Eras in Contrast

importance as corporate America realizes that each web is a *social system—and the social system is the factory*. Science has brought an explosion of human understanding. This era will provide the insights necessary to build highly collaborative and productive social systems. As understanding grows, the inhumanity of the prior era will fade away. It is a win-win model, unlocking potential by blending the findings of modern science with age-old wisdom:

> Even in such technical lines as engineering, about 15% of one's financial success is due to one's technical knowledge, *and about 85% is due to skill in human engineering, to personality and the ability to lead people*. (emphasis added)

> —Dale Carnegie

Fortunately, we have been putting many building blocks in place. Diversity was a training ground that increased our awareness and sensitivity to others. Now we must add a new dimension to our interpersonal understanding by becoming aware of the social, cognitive, and emotional aspects of human collaboration. This growth in our human understanding will become a competitive advantage, as we leverage social intelligence to unleash strengths in others. Although the transition will be difficult, it will be far more difficult for countries deeply tied to the industrial mind-set where workers are just another type of machine—keep it running, and if it breaks down, discard it and get a new one. We are many steps ahead on the pathway to human-centric practices.

As in all changes, this transformation will require understanding, trust, and conviction. We must, therefore, move forward with confidence, recognizing that the emerging environment is hospitable and will sustain us until we reach a much better place. As Buckminster Fuller once said, "You never change things by fighting the existing reality. To change something, build a new model that makes the existing model obsolete." That is where we are today, in the *transition zone*: a place where a socially intelligent, servant leadership paradigm will finally begin to reproduce itself. We must work collectively to make sure the new model is seen, understood, and embraced—a set of memes that inaugurates a new enlightenment.

As is well known, cultural change is a complex, time-consuming undertaking. But here there is good news: Changing the focus from self to others is very powerful indeed.

> Self-absorption in all its forms kills empathy, let alone compassion. When we focus on ourselves, our world contracts as our problems and preoccupations loom large. But when we focus on others, our world expands. Our own problems drift to the periphery of the mind and so seem smaller, and we increase our capacity for connection—or compassionate action.
>
> —Daniel Goleman

Leading companies like Google understand that the only shortcut is talent, and they have therefore embraced and nurtured a creative and motivated workforce. Clearly, the winners of this unfolding era will be led by servants who understand how to unlock human potential. Satisfyingly, this understanding will rehumanize the workforce, launching productivity revolutions within corporations that shun selfishness and short-term thinking; those that refuse to embrace their professionals will compete in a race to the bottom.

To fuel this revolution, an explosion of human understanding has arrived on cue. Brain science has revealed how the human mind works, and decades of scientific research has shown how we think and feel. Winning companies will design collaborative cultures where prosocial and caring behaviors give way to positive social chemistry. Here the minds and emotions of the workers will literally flourish, unlocking desperately needed innovation. The hands no longer matter; instead, we will learn to cultivate work environments where the collective state of mind is productive. Nothing is more important.

A Quick Book Tour

Chapter 1, "A Shining Light: The Blind Spot Revealed," shows that an inflection point has truly arrived. Peter Drucker said the management challenge of the twenty-first century would be to increase the productivity of knowledge work and knowledge workers. In my years of leading turnaround transformations of failed and/or failing information technology (IT) organizations, the author saw how they shared frightful, dark climates where the energy was consumed by protective behaviors, not productive work. We have so much to learn. Using the analogy of robots in a factory, the chapter shows how dysfunctional our management practices are, with our in-depth knowledge of technology and so little knowledge of our most expensive and important tools: our people. It introduces the need for servant leadership practices, unselfishness, and prosocial behaviors focused on the needs of others, and the importance of relegating toxic leadership practices to the past because they destroy the return on human capital.

Chapter 2, "Corporate America's IT Organization: Failure Is All Too Common," examines the history of corporate IT failure. Decades of IT project failure and underperformance are reviewed to underscore the fact that this is a long-standing problem. In fact, when compared to how much the performance of our technology (computers, storage, etc.) has increased during this same time period, we are left to wonder: How did one improve so much, while the other so little? Sixty years into the information era, IT remains a marriage of necessity, not love, in traditional corporate America. Failures are worse than publicly admitted, and, when one looks closely, we see these failures are a failure of management, not the IT organizations. If management would just embrace its people, instead of external experts and silver bullets, IT would perform well. Management can turn around troubled organizations by acquiring, growing, and retaining talent, and relying on human factors like, trust, meaningful teamwork, and real cross-functional collaboration to create reliable execution and project delivery. A quick review of the silver bullets shows that the solution to IT failure will be found by applying human-centric practices and understanding within the corporation.

Chapter 3, "Man as Machine: A Social Pathology," examines the root cause of persistent IT failure. A trip back to the industrial era reveals a mind-set that turned craftsmen into machines, where organizations became devoid of emotion, corporate Easter Islands whose workers stare blankly into space. The management ethos that created these cold, industrial settings flowed into our present era, so the blank stares remain, and through the blank stares we find a root cause: antisocial, selfish behaviors create environments that are toxic to cognitive productivity, where the human infrastructure literally shuts down, causing labor burn rates and costs to explode as productivity plummets.

It is a paradox, but it is real. Our human resource practices remain primitive but, as clearly shown, they perpetuate themselves, awaiting a movement outside the corporation to ignite the flames of productive change.

In Chapter 4, "The Unseen Art and Emotion of IT: The Acme Inc. Philharmonic Orchestra: Knowledge as Notes, Leaders as Conductors, Programmers as Composers," we take a detailed look at the hidden inner world of IT projects, where mind and emotion are the tools of a conceptual and emotional reality shared by artistic co-creators who have to deeply collaborate to turn concepts into reality. It is within this inner realm of the mind where alignment—conceptual unity—is found, but only if there is a high degree of social cohesion to facilitate the unfettered exchange of information. Here we examine how the process-based models and controls of the industrial factory are inadequate, because people-based potential can be unlocked only by leveraging the human factors to animate the workers. Using music as a metaphor, we see how composers (programmers) use a variety of instruments (programming and design tools) to create unique works (solutions); here we begin to look at the challenges of leading the IT orchestra, where the business cannot see the hidden inner reality, where the instruments keep changing, where hyperspecialization is the norm, and where human-centric practices are the unused levers of an unfolding era. When professionals are treated as mere parts, the financial impact is dramatic.

This is clearly shown in Chapter 5, "Case Study: An Unproductive State of Mind: Toxic Leadership and Its Aftermath." Because every software development project creates unique output, we have not been able to measure the productivity impact of different management practices. Finding a case study that looks at toxic leadership and its aftermath was a challenge, but the author did uncover one. IT is all about working social, so here we see how socially corrosive behaviors impede the complex human collaboration required to build a solution and the bottom-line impact such toxicity creates. Failure is a distinctly human drama, and in this case study, an unsuspecting group of professionals quickly go from celebrating success to sharing an unfolding disaster. The casualties are real; the names have been changed to protect the guilty.

Chapter 6, "What Are We Waiting For? Applied Science at Work," provides an academic research window through which the human factors of productivity are visible. Beginning with the Hawthorne experiments and culminating with research into neuroscience, we take a tour that shows how a leader can employ the human factors to unlock the productivity of any organization and how an individual contributor can positively impact the team he or she is on. Find out how your expectations drive results both up and down; see how empathy and compassion evolved as tools that you can use with great effect today; understand why organizational citizenship behavior should be embraced to drive higher performance; find out how the limbic system shuts down the human infrastructure if threats exist in the workplace; see how shared emotional needs drive productivity; find out how mirror neurons form a physiological connection between every member of a team; and, last, learn how the human infrastructure has physical limitations based on how it evolved. All of this matters immensely when your factory floor is powered by minds and emotions.

Leaders must develop expertise in how to operate the "human equipment," just like any costly tool provided to them. In Chapter 7, "Empathy and Compassion: The Socially Cohesive and Resilient Organization," we explore how both these emotions are powerful drivers of productivity. The chapter recommends using the overarching term *caring* to describe them, as it is more acceptable in corporate environments that are still hostile toward feeling. We discover how empathy and compassion are extroverted social emotions that help reduce stress through a process of noticing and responding. We also explore the role of toxic handlers, individuals who quietly raise the productive capacity of the organization by deeply caring about others, thereby elevating organizational mood. Workers touched in this way become both present and productive. With employee engagement at all-time lows, and stress causing an enormous drop in group productivity, showing concern for others is more important than ever. This chapter explains how and why, enabling you to improve your effectiveness and that of your organization.

Since great IT is all about productive thought and meaningful social interaction, Chapter 8 is titled "Designing a Collaborative Social System: Working Social: How the Right Culture Unlocks Productivity." Here you learn how culture unlocks productivity and how the collective thoughts and emotions of hyperspecialized professionals can be choreographed to produce a great solution. Both the social environment and social interaction are integral to IT, but productive harmony is unleashed only when the silos, walls, and cubicles that workers hide behind are taken down. As the saying goes, in unity, there is strength; effective collaboration frees creative solutions to nagging issues that block the path forward, lightening a heavy workload. You can increase both the speed and quality of thousands of individual interactions by applying what is recommended here.

In Chapter 9, "The Social Compact: Organizational Citizenship Behavior," we look at how organizational citizenship behavior is an essential tool. Corporations shape how their customer service representatives interact with clients, constantly reinforcing the importance of being sensitive to each client's needs so that levels of customer intimacy rise. Why not teach professional intimacy, so employees understand how to productively collaborate with their fellow workers? Here we take a look at a set of guidelines you can employ to create productive social interaction. None of them is revolutionary, yet all are highly productive because toxic, antisocial, and even neutral behavior is the norm. Your upside is significant, and it costs very little to magnify teamwork and collaboration. From my experience, when employees reflexively help one another, organizational effectiveness quickly improves due to stronger working relationships and shared institutional knowledge. Read this chapter to understand how you can give your organization a boost.

By the time you have gotten this far, you will have gained valuable understanding about how to build a high-performing organization. But great leadership that is prosocial and authentic is essential, and when it comes to IT, nothing is more important than the topic of Chapter 10, titled "The Servant Leader: Prosocial and Authentic." Unselfishness is an especially productive leadership skill because it enables you to focus on the needs of others, thus unlocking their potential. As you read through this chapter, you discover the leadership behaviors that draw teams together, enliven an organization, and animate a great performance. Certainly the desires of individuals matter, but IT leadership is ultimately about making teams great and leaving individual desires subservient to the needs of the group. As noted in this chapter, there are many successful leadership styles; yet the research shows that a caring culture led by someone in the service of his or her people is highly productive. Perhaps nothing has broader productivity implications. Tone at the top is a real force.

Chapter 11 digs into an area that underpins successful teamwork and collaboration: "Social and Emotional Intelligence: Organizational Canvas Meets the Social Paintbrush." After a brief review of what the academic research shows, this chapter covers these skills and how they can be applied. Ultimately, reading the emotional state of individuals and the collective organization provides a window into how productive the social climate is and invites you to make it better. Pulling the right emotional levers creates a more productive atmosphere, stronger social cohesion, and improved collaboration. The chapter contains a list of suggested actions to employ to improve social sentiment, thus energizing the performance of your coworkers, team, or division. People are hired for their IQ but then fired most often for lack of emotional intelligence. Honing your skills in this area will pay both a personal and an organizational dividend.

If you have built an environment where projects are done on time, the next milestone is leveraging the talent to create competitive advantage. There is never enough top-line growth, so unleashing innovation is imperative. The best way to accomplish this is to employ the proven techniques outlined in Chapter 12, "Designing an Innovative Culture." Great outcomes are not the result of chance but of a series of wise decisions that deliver desired results. Much research has been done on innovation, yet it remains elusive for most companies. Yours does not have to be one of them. If you employ the practices outlined here and are sensitive to the role of culture, you can improve your outcomes. Certainly, making innovation an organizational imperative is important, but that is only the beginning. Approaching the problem in a practical, holistic manner, as explained in this chapter, will continuously move the needle.

With innovation cooking and a wellspring of productivity flowing because you have successfully stirred the dormant potential of both individuals and teams, you must now relentlessly invigorate your talent base. Nothing is more productive than a small, tightly knit group of high-aptitude professionals with deep institutional knowledge. These are assets, not expenses, and, as assets, they must be nurtured and developed. This is where Chapter 13, "Workforce Planning: Maximizing the Productivity of Your Talent—Today and Tomorrow," enters the equation. Building a high-performing organization is critical; refining it, growing it, and ensuring you maximize the productivity of your talent, today and tomorrow, is an overarching responsibility. Here you find a high-level methodology that is both strategic and tactical; see how it encompasses a cycle of activities; and understand that workforce planning is an ongoing process, no different from managing expenses, contracts, and system availability. Talent remains the only shortcut. It is time to embrace it.

Our journey together so far has been productive, and we have seen many things. Chapter 14, "How to Successfully Transform Your Organization: Putting It All Together," pulls everything together so you can apply the insights and techniques shared in this book in your own organization. This chapter lays out a holistic approach, including practices beyond the scope of this book, so you can see the big picture. Great IT has many variables that extend beyond culture, talent, and leadership, but the human factors intertwine around everything. This chapter contains a simple recipe that the author has used with great success, covering organizational design, strategy, tone at the top, governance, culture, talent, the importance of growing experience, and IT best practices in context of the human factors covered in this book. It is a handy reference that simplifies an inherently complex process so that you can thoughtfully transform your area and win.

As you travel on from here, you will find that the journey itself is the reward. Nothing is more gratifying than unlocking greatness in others. As you will experience, the greatest journey lies within.

Note

1. *The American Heritage Dictionary of the English Language* (4th ed.) (New York, NY: Houghton Mifflin, 2000).

CHAPTER 1

A Shining Light

The Blind Spot Revealed

> Humanity's most valuable assets have been the non-conformists. Were it not for the non-conformists, he who refuses to be satisfied to go along with the continuance of things as they are, and insists upon attempting to find new ways of bettering things, the world would have known little progress, indeed.
>
> —JOSIAH WILLIAM GITT

Corporate life is quickly accelerating toward an inflection point. Many people talk of feeling "it": an uneasiness about the future and a palpable sense that a momentous shift of some kind is taking shape in the business world around us. Basic industries, and portions of our knowledge work, continue to move offshore, leaving a vacuum that must be filled. Even worse, selfishness and greed have grown like cancers, destroying iconic corporations and tearing at the social fabric of once great and caring companies. A house divided ultimately fails.

This inflection point represents an onrushing shift. As in past shifts, new businesses will assuredly spring up to replace those that fail or are commoditized. As the twenty-first century unfolds, knowledge workers will staff these new businesses, and their productivity will become the primary management challenge for America and the developed world.

Peter Drucker saw this coming:

> The most important, and indeed the truly unique contribution of management in the 20th century was the fifty-fold increase in the productivity of the MANUAL WORKER in manufacturing.
>
> The most important contribution management needs to make in the twenty-first century is similarly to increase the productivity of KNOWLEDGE WORK and the KNOWLEDGE WORKER.

The most valuable assets of a 20th-century company were its production equipment. The most valuable asset of a twenty-first-century institution, whether business or non-business, will be its *knowledge workers* and their *productivity*.[1]

A Race to the Bottom

But this new dawn remains just a glimmer of light. In today's information economy, a key lever of value creation—collaborative information technology (IT) projects staffed by knowledge workers—still fails or underperforms at an alarming rate. Decades of research, trillions of dollars of experience, and pundits galore, but we still have deplorable success rates and limited business satisfaction.

Although we have effectively created the raw materials of this unfolding era—semiconductors, storage, networking, software, process models, and lots of knowledge—we have not been successful at inventing a postindustrial leadership model to leverage its most important ingredient: the knowledge worker.

Something as essential as the productivity of our twenty-first-century workforce remains poorly understood. Knowledge doubles every few years, while our ability to store and retrieve information doubles every 18 months, but our ability to unfailingly leverage knowledge and experience across teams of highly skilled individuals remains stalled. As an economy, we must learn to reliably turn knowledge into opportunity. Today, teams of individuals do that; today, our value creation track record, as far as IT is concerned, is very poor because corporate America has ignored the social and emotional levers of productivity. We have been consumed with "self," insensitive to the needs and feelings of others. The industrial era allowed us to master things, not people. Fortunately, this leadership blind spot will quickly disappear under the lights of applied science and human-centric leadership practices.

As we journey farther into the information economy, we look back and see that industrial-era capitalism has reached an evolutionary endpoint: double-entry accounting from the fifteenth century, process-focused models rooted in industrial engineering, command-and-control leadership hierarchies, and the commoditization of workers within a global labor pool. At this juncture we have perfected economies of scale, continuous process improvement, quality engineering, and supply chain management, which have in turn created the likes of Walmart, General Electric, IBM, and Ford—all leading players in their markets. But make no mistake, the endless pursuit of efficiency pits them in a human capital race to the bottom.

It becomes more difficult and costly to constantly squeeze further leverage out of a process-focused mentality and culture. Businesses both great and small have been created, and great wealth has been produced, yet we now see the undesirable consequences of our process orientation and our need to count everything: the dehumanization of the workforce. As Einstein said, "Not everything that counts can be measured; and not everything that can be measured counts." Just imagine if we had to quantify the return on investment of a hug?

Because of this dehumanization, our most valuable asset of all—our knowledge workers—are disillusioned, and corporate is unraveling. We have expunged all emotion and feeling so that our human assets more closely resemble industrial robots (which, by the way, come from the Czech word *robota*, meaning drudgery, or slavelike labor). Dilbert resonates far and wide.

The physical means of production—computers, corporate infrastructure, labor, and process methodologies—are now easily copied. As a result, a downward pricing spiral is in motion. Businesses are effortlessly replicated in low-cost countries such that supply often exceeds demand, technology improvements endlessly lower the cost of entry for new competitors, and the victory of capitalism continuously brings new countries and labor into a global free market. Industrial capitalism, we see, has itself become a commodity.

Human Understanding Enters the Workplace

Psychological research and neurological studies of the brain reveal that the mind is highly modular, and intelligence is a kaleidoscope of capabilities. Authors and researchers like Daniel Goleman, Martin Seligman, Howard Gardner, Joseph Ledoux, and countless others, are allowing us to see ourselves in the rainbow of a new light.[2] As with any emerging area of understanding, there are camps and debate. But the time has come for this research, and what it reveals, to be applied in business, creating a new branch of management science. The current body of research makes a strong case for a leadership style where the happiness and emotional well-being of workers must be a top priority, not just in thought but also in deed. We are entering a time where leaders will become the servants and productivity will flow like a wellspring.

It seems clear that Drucker's challenge will be fully answered with a warmer, human-centric approach to management that is discernible in today's research concerning mind and emotion. Literally, we are on the precipice of a productivity revolution, not unlike what was unleashed by Frederick Taylor[3] and the Efficiency Movement. Our focus must now shift to building and managing productive social systems where our professionals can flourish; we must ensure that our "talent infrastructure" is operating as well as our networks and equipment; we must educate our leaders to understand the human factors, and apply them, just as they apply Six Sigma and process standards like COBIT and Information Technology Infrastructure Library (ITIL); we must finally heed the advice of

Abraham Maslow[4] and Frederick Hertzberg,[5] who counseled that humanism was needed in the workplace.

But today, leaders are uninformed about the wealth of findings uncovered by decades of research into the most important part of every company: its talent. In IT, although 60 to 70 percent of operating expense goes to talent, that talent remains heavily underutilized.

Imagine a factory where 65 percent of your operating costs were for complex equipment, yet:

- You don't have a single operators' manual.
- You have no idea if it will work successfully the next time you use it.
- You can't track return on investment for each unit.
- You have no idea how to measure and tune the equipment's performance.
- The people responsible for networking your equipment together have never been trained to do this.
- There is a wealth of available research that describes how to optimize the use of your equipment, yet everyone ignores it.
- Your equipment is constantly replaced with less expensive units, even though the existing equipment has been painstakingly programmed over years, at great expense, with all of the institutional knowledge.
- Your equipment has to be networked together to create output, yet there is no wiring diagram, and no one has any idea if the connections are working.
- Each piece of your equipment is unique, yet your managers mistakenly believe the machines are interchangeable parts and move them whenever they feel it is necessary.
- Every year you invest money to add new capabilities to your equipment, but no one tracks this investment, so the increased value is ignored when replacement is evaluated.

If you run an IT organization (or most any organization for that matter), all of this is true. Even though the bulk of the expense is on talent, we have no human capital accounting; most of the research into social psychology and neuroscience is ignored; and we invest the bulk of our energy into maintaining and improving our computing environments, software, networks, and storage. In that case, we know every patch and configuration level for every server and device, yet we track almost nothing about our people. Our focus is unbalanced: The server is $5,000 and the database administrator is $100,000. We must be expert at both.

Shouldn't we invest more time to optimize our talent infrastructure, given that it is the past, present, and future source of our competitive advantage?

Shouldn't we know vastly more than we do about our human capital? Shouldn't we understand the opportunity cost of so inefficiently managing our human capital? Shouldn't we eliminate this blind spot?

Yes, we should. Corporate America has simply failed to create a working environment where people count. According to research by Robert Hurely, published in 2006, roughly half of all managers surveyed did not trust their leaders (and the numbers are no doubt higher now), based on a survey of 450 executives across 30 companies.[6]

We Have Been Taught Not to See or Feel

Quite simply, our industrial past enabled us to perfect the use of the computing infrastructure but left us blind to the human infrastructure. The management beliefs and practices that caused this blindness have flowed from one generation of leaders to the next, forming an unbroken chain of inheritance back to Frederick Taylor and our industrial past. We involuntarily embrace the operational, organizational, and administrative norms that emanate from a time where the focus was unfeeling machines, assembly lines, and production processes and controls and where the sensations and emotions of the workers were inconsequential to the bottom line. This culturally transmitted blindness causes a condition where our *knowledge workers* and the *social systems* that bind them together are invisible, because *we have been taught not to see them*.

The source of this blindness is not just work but our educational system as well. All the way through school, we were *taught to think but not to feel*. People often say "I think I feel" instead of "I feel." Consequently, no one has learned to feel, understand, and productively use their emotions, let alone see them in others. It is an enormous blind spot because emotion is critical to both personal and professional success, especially if you become a leader, at which point social intelligence is a crucial tool. No one can flourish without fully understanding themselves and their impact on others. Although we live and work in a world driven by emotion, most people are left to discover it on their own.

Humans also have limited conscious capacity. The world of early humans was a very dangerous place, so we are wired to focus on a few critical things. Think about how an easily distracted mind would have made humans a much easier prey. This concentrated focus is clearly a survival skill.

As a result, most people today can concentrate on something if you tell them to. A famous psychological study called the Invisible Gorilla shows the strength of this phenomenon. In this experiment, a group of observers are asked to carefully watch a three-and-a-half-minute movie and count how many times a basketball is passed between a group of players. During the short film, a large man in a gorilla suit walks right across the screen, stops, waves, and then exits the scene. You would think no one could miss him, but half the observers do. Why? They are doing what humans do very well: focusing on precisely what they have been asked to focus on. The human factors of productivity are the gorilla in our room, and these are equally large and waving right at us from the research.

Unfortunately, the behavioral and psychological aspects of social collaboration clash with the insensitive nature of our leadership style. Knowledge work is incompatible with the inhumane practices of the industrial era, causing today's low returns on human capital and high levels of disengagement. The world of work has changed, but our practices have not.

Unlocking Human Potential

Social systems designed for productive human interaction must assume the same position that assembly lines held during the industrial revolution. To lead these contemporary "production lines," a generation of prosocial leaders who selflessly focus on the needs of others will step to the forefront and set the pent-up human potential free; they will understand that it is more valuable to unlock productivity than to contain it; and they will artfully shape behavior and emotion so that human interaction becomes *socioproductive*[7] *by design*. The emotional dam will be broken, and higher cognitive functions, so constrained by emotionally toxic environments, will begin to flow freely.

We need to care about our talent and nurture its potential. In the industrial era, we worshiped our machines and all they could do for us, because we controlled them, and understood every productivity driver. Americans stood in awe of mechanization and what it accomplished, not unlike how we today worship our devices. We always marveled at our power to produce mass quantities of physical goods at ever-decreasing unit costs; at our ability to control and manage output; and at our ability to leverage process, counting and measuring everything. Now we must become equally enamored with the human infrastructure and understand the research that shows how knowledge workers actually produce something. (In Chapter 4, I show how IT is more art and emotion than engineering, but the emotional side, the *art*, has been overlooked, with damaging consequences.)

Another reason we have overlooked the human factors of knowledge worker productivity is that they are not easily quantified. Trust is a critical lever of productivity when groups of knowledge workers collaborate—yet it is ascribed no value and isn't measured; blame and other antisocial behaviors stimulate the amygdala, impairing a worker's ability to think by creating fear and stress, but because we cannot measure the productivity impact, this detrimental behavior is ignored; transparency and honesty create safe environments where people can relax, collaborate freely, and solve problems, but the benefit is tough to quantify, so it is ignored. The list goes on and on.

I have walked into organizations where a toxic, antisocial leader had done the equivalent of powering down the network and data center. The human infrastructure had literally lost power—emotionally drained, disengaged, and depressed—the social network was frayed, and information moved slowly between people, if at all; the factory of minds and emotions was barely operating. You could see the low energy in the workers' lifeless faces, disconnected from their coworkers by pervasive and palpable distrust, going through the motions, the bonds with management severed. On paper, more hours of labor were being consumed than ever—attendance was good. Yet, in a thought-based business, presence doesn't matter, only a productive state of mind does. Our human resource practices are so inadequate to the task.

Dawn of a New Productivity Model

We must embark on a mission to ensure that human capital is the best understood, most appreciated, most productive tool in the workplace, not the least—collectively unleashing an era lush with understanding and compassion. People aren't interchangeable parts, and they probably should have never been used this way, but it happened, and to a large degree they remain *human resources* (just another resource like capital, raw materials, energy, etc.) today. Viewing them as parts, or resources, has unintended consequences as it encourages selfishness. *If you are just an interchangeable part, then you don't matter. And if you don't matter, then I will focus on my needs, not yours.* Deeper understanding about the corrosive nature of our practices will launch a productivity revolution and, in the process, human understanding in the workplace will be seen not as a love-in but as the most efficient and productive way to increase the return on human capital.

The human factors of productivity, shaped by millions of years of evolution, are central to collaboration and knowledge worker output. We are on the verge of a breakthrough—an inflection point where the unseen becomes suddenly visible. The layer of human productivity drivers that sits above the process layer bequeathed by the industrial revolution is manifesting itself and will drive corporate America to transform from a cold, process-focused entity to one infused with the warmth of human understanding.

I see it happening, glimmers of light visible in many areas. Judging by the warm reaction I get to my talks and the calls I get to come in and speak to organizations, I conclude one thing: There is both a recognition of and thirst for an antidote to the feelings created when professionals are treated as interchangeable parts. *Trust, collaboration, sharing, caring, empathy, compassion, unselfishness, prosocial behavior, humor, meaning, harmony, openness, social acceptance, mutual respect, and transparency,* flowing within a *blame-free* culture, are powerful sources of competitive advantage. They heal emotionally unhealthy environments and allow the productivity potential to be reached and IT workers to flourish. These are the humanistic drivers of a neuroscientific/behavioral productivity model evident in today's research and proven absolutely effective across the turnaround transformations I led.

As for leaders, research shows they need to be authentic, trustworthy, empathetic, selfless, caring, upbeat (mood is contagious), capable of giving work meaning, possessing an ability to speak with candor (openness) and a desire to maintain open lines of communication; they must model prosocial behavior because behavior is contagious (people don't do what you say, they do what you do!); and, last, they must clearly see the big picture, as this awareness enables them to communicate the importance of the work rather than just the assignment. None of this is to suggest there aren't great leaders—there are. But not many have embraced and used this new understanding. Great ones can be greater still.

When you create an organization with these characteristics, people are happy, motivated, upbeat, and highly productive, displaying a high degree of social cohesion and sharing information freely. The more they share and help one another, the faster work moves, especially if you have cultivated deep and intimate institutional experience and retained it, because it is so costly to acquire. Any good leader in IT who came up from the trenches has witnessed the incredible productivity, and solutions, generated by enthusiastic employees with deep experience and high aptitude. They are fast, consistently 10 times faster, according to the research.[8]

Unfortunately, all too often, these talented, highly experienced workers are traded for junior offshore resources, as if strong talent with deep institutional experience were a commodity. It isn't. High aptitude talent is always in short supply, and great talent is rarer still. Once lost, experience has to be regrown; but with commodity talent, the experience develops slowly and then is lost again and again through turnover. How uninformed these practices are! Knowledge workers are assets, not expenses, and like any asset, they should be grown.

Economic theory and most business practice see manual workers as a cost. To be productive, knowledge workers must be considered a capital asset. Costs need to be controlled and reduced. Assets need to be made to grow.

—PETER DRUCKER

Working Social

To me, this breakthrough has arrived and is fully visible. To realize the full benefit, corporations must transform their cultural focus from "self" (selfish) to "group" (unselfish) and at long last unlock the value trapped within today's dysfunctional social systems. Reward systems must evolve from "What's in it for me?" and "I win, you lose" to "What's in it for us?" Socially corrosive forces must be replaced by sensitive, outwardly focused cultures that eliminate the insensitivity handed down from the industrial era. And, at long last, trust must be recognized by corporations as the glue that tightly bonds individuals together so that groups of knowledge workers can reliably create value. Most important, antisocial leaders who destroy trust must embrace new behaviors or be pushed aside into an individual contributor role, or out the door.

Consequently, the leading corporations of tomorrow will embrace prosocial behavior and caring cultures as the new means of production—the modern equivalent of a fast and efficient assembly line. These prosocial enterprises will focus on increasing the frequency and value of truly collaborative interaction, and will seek a new generation of leaders who are socially intelligent and unselfish enough to design, build and manage a social system. High-return, high-frequency interactions need to become the rule, not the exception.

As this new paradigm emerges, we will go back to the future, finding within ourselves the social skills that formed millions of years ago as early humans evolved into social animals. All workers share a common evolutionary heritage, rooted in tribes, culture, and social behavior—a core part of our being that enables us to very naturally form a social unit where the whole is greater than the sum of the parts. The good news, based on my experience, is that today's cold, dysfunctional, and unproductive social environments snap quickly back to their organic shape when a caring, prosocial, and authentic culture is created. They have been deformed, not destroyed.

Industrial management hierarchy will give way to a new organizational paradigm, the *social hierarchy*, where teams become *social units*, the elementary building blocks of larger *social systems* (formerly departments), which in turn roll up to form a *social complex* (formerly division), the building blocks of the *social enterprise* (yes, driven for profit, but shared more equitably, because that is the most productive design).

In order for these social enterprises to operate efficiently, a social climate conducive to open interaction will become the design imperative. Leaders will embrace the human factors of productivity to enable high-return group interaction—with a constant emphasis on collective outcomes. Professionals will embrace *organizational citizenship behavior* (covered in depth in Chapter 9), thereby forming strong relationships, fully opening connections among contributors so that knowledge flows and collective thoughts and ideas are given meaningful expression. Understanding, gratitude, and outflowing concern for others (empathy and caring) will animate the social fabric of productivity, and people will no longer have to check their emotions at the door. The collective intelligence will be tapped to create new and exciting products and services, generating stronger and more sustainable returns on human capital and improved profitability.

The Social System Is the Factory

Each knowledge worker is a unique thread of talent, different from every other, with different cognitive abilities, behaviors, and emotional intelligence. But the great news is that we share emotional needs. It is these shared human factors of productivity that provide a framework we can embrace to drive engagement and organizational effectiveness. As noted, the human factors provide a whole new perspective on how to view the organization: Departments are actually social systems, where social skills and the social climate enable (or hinder) the formation of relationships and productivity.

Each social system is actually a loom upon which threads of mind and emotion are woven together to form teams; the tighter the weave, the greater the productivity. The individual threads of talent are held together by trust, forming a tightly knitted social fabric that accelerates the sharing of knowledge and experience between individuals and teams. Every thread that remains unwoven represents a significant loss of human capital. Unfortunately, few managers know how to build trust, while many are skilled at destroying it.

The more trust flourishes, the tighter the weave becomes, and the greater the strength of the social fabric holding the professionals together. Out of this unity grows meaningful teamwork and collaboration, a critical productivity driver of the postindustrial era. The social system is indeed the modern factory!

> The major replacement for the Taylor system will be self-directing teams of workers.
>
> —JOSEPH M. JURAN

Tight bonds will finally replace tentative connections, trust and caring will give way to harmony, and the highest form of social interaction will materialize as the social units gel into truly high-performing organizations. This is how you create organizational effectiveness in IT: Let high-value labor fluidly exchange thoughts and ideas within corporate cultures sensitively tuned to the needs of these producers. Done effectively, the smile index will signal that the "factory" is running well and the "machines" are operating at peak efficiency. Tools will emerge to track how investment turns into experience, helping to fine-tune the social climate so that the experience turns into value.

This new paradigm will be built on top of existing best practices (all of which are very important, and an indispensable foundation). Although collaboration is already valued, knowledge workers themselves are still viewed as "human resources" that must be process controlled to "maximize" productivity and reduce risk. They are merely "interchangeable parts" that turn inputs into outputs, performing manual activities within otherwise automated processes; our industrial heritage remains in the foreground, enforcing rigid, quantitative, process-centric management practices that cannot accommodate such abstract measures as emotion, bonds, feelings, harmony, trust, and meaning. Rather than confront them, we ignore them.

The productivity needs of this era of intense collaboration, hyperspecialization, creativity, lengthy time to competency, and emotionally driven productivity will cause us to broaden our view of what counts. In a *New York Times* article, "Do Happier People Work Harder?" the authors make reference to a Gallup poll that shows our workers are more disengaged than ever.[9] According to the article, Gallup's Healthways Well-Being Index is based on a daily poll of 1,000 adults since 2008. Americans feel worse about their jobs and work environments than they ever have before. It is estimated by Gallup that this disengagement crisis is costing the economy over $300 billion a year. That sum is truly staggering, and no doubt underestimated, when one realizes that a worker's number one desire is to be appreciated. This has shown up in exit interview statistics for years (i.e., people do not want to be treated like interchangeable parts). Social systems tuned to maximize human interaction must be viewed like the assembly lines and process controls that kicked the industrial revolution into high gear. To drive this "soft assembly," a generation of prosocial leaders will come to the forefront and set the pent-up human potential free. They will understand it is more valuable to unlock productivity than to contain it, so they will artfully shape people's behavior and sensitively influence emotion so that human interaction becomes *socioproductive*. The emotional dam will be broken.

Let the corporate social revolution begin! Its arrival will address the most prominent cause of IT project failure, an all-too-common occurrence, as highlighted in the next chapter, finally unlocking the knowledge worker productivity waiting to be tapped.

Notes

1. Peter Drucker, *Management Challenges for the 21st Century* (New York: Harper Collins, 1999). See "Knowledge-Worker Productivity," 135–159.
2. Daniel Goleman is an author, psychologist, science journalist, and lecturer who is most famous for his 1995 book *Emotional Intelligence* (New York: Bantam Books). That book sold over 5 million copies and brought the notion of EQ (Emotional Intelligence Quotient) versus

IQ (Intelligence Quotient) into the mainstream, although that topic had been written about and researched extensively prior to the release of Goleman's work.

3. Martin Seligman is the director of the Positive Psychology Center at the University of Pennsylvania. He is the author of numerous articles, newsletters, and the book *Flourish* (New York: Free Press, 2011).

4. Frederick Taylor was the first person to discover that work was worth studying. He launched the Efficiency Movement and ultimately management science. Taylorism had an enormous impact on work, and Taylor was confident that his efforts would lead to greater worker happiness and engagement because the understanding of process would make their jobs more interesting. In fact, Taylorism did just the opposite. Workers were reduced to interchangeable parts, and process control lowered the level of employee engagement by removing task control from jobs.

5. Abraham Maslow is a famous psychologist who served as the chair of the department of psychology at Brandeis University from 1951 to 1969. Today he is well known for his Hierarchy of Human Needs, although he published many books and articles on a variety of subjects. He was a humanist who believed that people should be happy and self-actualized, fulfilling more than their basic needs. Frederick Hertzberg is a psychologist who became famous for his writings on motivation. One of the first management articles I read was a *Harvard Business Review* piece by Hertzberg on motivator-hygiene theory that made a strong case that managers need to stop doing unproductive things in order to release the productivity potential of the organization. It always stuck with me and was an early influence on my orientation toward leadership. Hertzberg was widely published in the 1970s and 1980s.

6. Robert F. Hurley, "The Decision to Trust," *Harvard Business Review* (September 2006): 55–62.

7. *Socio-productive* as used in this book describes a work environment where the social chemistry and human interaction have been artfully designed to unlock the untapped human productivity potential that is freely available (waiting to be tapped) to corporations. Socio-productive practices increase the return on human capital.

8. Many studies have shown a 10× productivity factor between the best programmers and worst programmers, and between teams. See the work of Harlan Mills, who authored *Software Productivity*, published by Little, Brown in 1983. He personally achieved coding rates 10× the average today. Earlier studies by Sackman, Erikson, and Grant (1968) actually showed a 20× difference. These considerable differences in productivity were also shown by Bill Curtis (1981), whose research paper, "Substantiating Programmer Variability", revealed a 10× difference in capability on a debugging task. More recently, Tom DeMarco and Tim Lister showed the difference across teams in *Peopleware* (New York: Dorset House, 1999). The research is extensive and significant aptitude-driven performance differences hold true across professions as shown in other studies. In IT, team composition and the work environment are enormous drivers of productivity, in addition to aptitude, as discussed throughout this book.

9. Teresa Amabile and Steven Kramer, "Do Happier People Work Harder?" *New York Times.* Available at www.nytimes.com.

CHAPTER 2

Corporate America's IT Organization

Failure Is All Too Common

The truth you believe and cling to makes you unavailable to hear anything new.

—PEMA CHÖDRÖN

In the information technology (IT) profession, the actors change yet the failures remain the same. We remain ignorant of the human factors that drive knowledge worker productivity, with the most expensive, least understood resource being our talent. Although we have been funding large IT initiatives for over half a century, the bigger the investment, the more likely you will have a total write-off. We are unable to break free of a cultural model that embraces process warmly while coldly treating people, thus perpetuating a cycle of project failure in this human-centric, emotional endeavor. The lost productivity and wasted investment is a shameful waste of competitive resources. Realistically, factories that consistently produced such a low yield would have been shuttered long ago.

Corporate America's ignorance of the human factors of productivity, and our reliance on all things *unhuman*, has been long in the making. Henry Ford turned on the first moving assembly line in 1913 and established a revolution in the production of manufactured goods at Ford's Highland Park, Michigan, plant. By combining the moving assembly line, standardized components, and a range of resources, including steel, energy, rubber, and "human resources," Ford designed a step-by-step fabrication process that minimized his cost and maximized his output. The industrial revolution was under way, and its lessons still inform our decision making.

Today's knowledge work was cast in these industrial molds. Like the factories of yore, IT projects use defined processes (software development methodologies) and tools (computers and software) to produce finished goods. This is a knowledge worker "assembly line," and its function is to create the products, services, and infrastructure that run today's corporations. Unlike the industrial era, however, this assembly line creates intellectual property rather than physical goods. Although not immediately obvious, we have replaced the assembly line with a *social system*.

Individuals working in the IT industry sense that business and technology are stuck in an incompatible relationship yet, like an old married couple, they accept their routine. The quantitative personality of Mr. Business clashes with the artistic nature of his IT spouse, even though they find one another fascinating and rely heavily on each other. Consequently, they bicker often and would undoubtedly separate if divorce weren't so costly and the mutual dependence wasn't so deep. IT is inherently about *working social*. Our poor results reflect how our lack of understanding of the human infrastructure impedes the complex human collaboration that underpins the information economy's growth and highlights corporate America's inability to reliably lead large teams of knowledge workers to greatness. Our collective blindness to distinctly human factors like emotion and social intelligence reveals itself in the ongoing struggle between our desires and our outcomes. The current state of corporate IT cries out for a human solution rather than another silver bullet.

I have spent most of my management career in IT leading turnaround transformations of failed or poorly performing IT organizations. This role gave me a powerful vantage point from which to see how pervasive IT failure really is—even inside organizations that had reasonably good public reputations in the industry. As you come onboard, reality is starkly visible: teams of unhappy people; pervasive project failure; a lack of transparency, such that every "red" project has a "green" status; low morale with the spirit of the workers broken; an absence of trust; high turnover causing a dangerous and extremely unproductive brain drain; and a sense of betrayal that permeates the social chemistry.

Given my personal experience, IT failure is pervasive and much higher than traditional corporations are willing to admit to. Yes, there are success stories, but you find these inside leading companies, like Google and Apple, that put a high premium on talent, nurturing a culture where the best and brightest can flourish. They are the exception, not the rule.

Still Broken after All These Years . . .

IT's roots are deep. The invention of the first electronic computer in 1945 (ENIAC) kicked off the information era in the United States, and from there it spread to the world. Out of the ashes of World War II, we took baby steps into the new age of knowledge work.

In the early 1950s, computers quickly found their way into business, although the initial deployments were highly specialized and of limited use.

But the industry evolved extraordinarily swiftly. A mere 20 years later, in 1964, IBM introduced the first modern business computer, the OS 360, with a full line of peripheral devices and a multitasking operating system (the OS) that a development team of over 1,000 people created. The world of business was changed forever. Given that failure is all too common, how have we progressed through the decades? Let's take a trip through time and see.

1964

The OS 360 endeavor was the largest and most successful software development effort up until this time. But the displeasure with IT was evident even then. Frederick Brooks, the manager of the OS 360 team in 1964, wrote, "[T]he product was late, it took more memory than planned, the costs were several times the estimate, and it did not perform very well until several releases after the first."[1] Brooks also wrote in the preface to *The Mythical Man Month* that "this book is the belated answer to Tom Watson's [IBM's chairman] probing question as to why programming is hard to manage."

The use of the word *probing* relates a sense of the intensity with which Watson questioned his managers. The product development cycle that spawned the OS 360 and launched the world into standardized business computing was a bet-the-ranch effort. Going three times over budget, on a project of that size and a bet of that magnitude, spawned many difficult questions. And, like low-fat food, none of the answers was very satisfying. But the social climate was warm, as Tom Watson cared deeply about his workers (unlike today).

Since this inflexion point, almost 60 years have elapsed. Today we find the same probing questions are still being asked. Unquestionably, we understand much more than we did then, so the answers are more eloquent, scientific, and elaborate—yet they are no more satisfying to the heads of our corporations.

1994

The Standish Group (www.standishgroup.com) has been studying IT project success and failure rates since 1994. It regularly publishes new studies based on updated data. The title of these research studies is CHAOS, an aptly chosen name that reflects the feelings of many inside and outside the industry. Although the trend is positive, the data are still very poor overall. Corporate IT just doesn't perform very well.

I found the original 1994 Standish Report online so that I can reference it, although I had downloaded it years ago.[2] Here are some of the findings from this report:

- In the United States, we spend more than $250 billion each year on IT application development of approximately 175,000 projects.

- The Standish Group research shows a staggering 31.1 percent of projects will be canceled before they ever get completed. Further results indicate 52.7 percent of projects will cost 189 percent of their original estimates. The cost of these failures and overruns are just the tip of the proverbial iceberg. The lost opportunity costs are not measurable, but could easily be in the trillions of dollars.
- Based on this research, The Standish Group estimates that in 1995 American companies and government agencies will spend $81 billion for canceled software projects.
- On the success side, the average is only 16.2 percent for software projects that are completed on time and on budget. In the larger companies, the news is even worse: Only 9 percent of their projects come in on time and on budget. And, even when these projects are completed, many are no more than a mere shadow of their original specification requirements.

2000

By 2000, we see some improvement in the numbers, yet failure remains staggering. Based on the 2001 Standish *Extreme Chaos* report,[3] 77 percent of all projects can be considered failures for one reason or another—which, remarkably, is a statistical improvement from 1994.

This number breaks into two groups: *failed* and *challenged*. The failures account for almost one-quarter of all projects (23 percent) and represent those efforts that were stopped prior to completion. Another 49 percent were challenged, which reflects projects that were delivered with significant problems: way over budget and a limited feature set versus what was promised.

In terms of unproductive capital, we are talking in the range of hundreds of billions of dollars. These are enormous numbers in their own right, but they pale into insignificance when you consider what value could have been created had all of this investment been maximized. What if these initiatives were not only on time and on budget but if just half the teams had been high performing—in a state of flow? Then the extrapolation is truly staggering.

Standish, by the way, is in the business of helping companies achieve better IT results. It uses the studies to find the root causes of failure and recommends best practice processes to improve success rates. There is debate about the validity and accuracy of the numbers since Standish tracks success versus original estimates. No matter, IT failure is real, and underdelivery is common.

2002

By 2002, the great Internet and Y2K booms are behind us. The economy is slipping more deeply into recession and the housing bubble is just beginning to take off. Although IT was revered during the great Nasdaq bull market and Internet bubble, no one is happy. The feeling remains the same today, but looking back at a McKinsey article titled "Transforming IT," we find:

> After spending more than $1.2 trillion on information technology products and services during the late 1990s, companies are slashing their IT budgets. In today's harsh climate, pressure to meet current earnings inspires much of this cost cutting, but many executives, believing that *their organizations gained little or no value from some of the systems installed during the great technology binge, are reluctant to send good money after bad.*[4]

The Internet boom was overhyped and led to mal-investment, as companies pushed forward with poorly thought-out strategies, compelled by market pressure to "do something important." At the same time, Y2K was for the most part driven by vendors, who pushed costly solutions into corporate IT. The estimates I received from many vendors at the time were ridiculous, so my teams chose to lead the efforts themselves for a fraction of the cost. I trusted my internal experts, who came up with realistic estimates based on intimate institutional knowledge—they were right; the vendors were wrong. This was a great example of the self-serving nature of the vendor marketplace, which stoked the fire and milked the situation. Many IT executives bought into the hype and became *very important* for that moment in time. No wonder executive management ended up dissatisfied.

2011

Figure 2.1 shows the customer perception of projects for the insurance industry, based on a Gartner research paper.[5]

Outstanding Success	23%	
Somewhat Successful	53%	
Somewhat Disappointing	17%	77%
Not Successful	7%	

Figure 2.1   Project Success Rates: Customer Perception
Source: Gartner: IT Key Metrics Data, 2011.

What is clear is that 77 percent of the projects led to some level of disappointment. Even though we have been refining how projects get done for 60 years, less than a quarter of the projects in this study were considered an outstanding success.

2012

McKinsey released very alarming findings based on a review of 5,400 projects.[6] The study looked at projects over $15 million, and found these were, on average, 45 percent over budget but delivered 56 percent less value than predicted. These findings were true across industries. As noted by the authors, the collective "cost overrun was $66 billion, more than the GDP of Luxembourg." Most concerning was their finding that 17 percent of the projects actually put the company at risk. These so called "black swan" events occur with greater frequency than would be expected and match or exceed those experienced on complex tunnel and bridge projects. Imagine that. No one has ever tracked how many companies have failed because they could not get IT working, but my experience indicates it is a big number.

The consistent underperformance of IT leaves a strong impression. In fact, in late summer 2011, I was having breakfast with Mark Lewis, the then head of IBM's Global Insurance practice. We met fairly regularly, and he had great insights because he frequently spoke with corporate chief executives. During breakfast he said he had recently returned from a meeting with over 50 chief executives from around the globe and one sentiment was held in common: "Our IT organizations do not perform well."

Not much has changed. Looking at the data and trends over many years, I draw a few conclusions, supported fully by my own experience:

- All too often, the only debate about investments in IT projects is not whether they will be a success or failure but the degree of failure.
- Dating back to the very origins of modern software development in the 1960s, project outcomes are questioned and dissatisfaction reigns.
- Success is not prominent. I tried finding a study of IT industry success that shows how great the industry runs and how wonderful sentiment is—but I gave up looking. Pundits offer many solutions but have few results.
- Large projects still fail or underperform regularly. In speaking with many senior people in the business, if you only include projects that cost $10 million or more, the results are grim. If you compare expectations to deliverables, it is easy to see why chief executives are unhappy.

Unfortunately, the Truth Is Worse

From my 29 years in IT leadership positions, it is very clear that neither corporations nor academia has an accurate picture of the financial magnitude of the failures. Four factors contribute to this positive bias:

1. **The internal numbers are understated.** The executives who initiated and sold many of the largest failures also shaped the perception of the outcome and the cost. Anyone in IT will tell you how many times he or she has seen a collective declaration of victory, when by any measure a development effort was a complete bust. Ultimately, reputations are at stake and managing perception is critical. More important, if data are provided to external sources, they are collected, massaged, and then circulated for further correction and approval.

   Corporations always put their best foot forward, so lipstick is put on the pig before it is paraded in front of the viewing stand. Unquestionably, statistics are appropriately massaged prior to release. Otherwise, they are not provided at all.

2. **Corporations broadcast successes, not failures.** Companies are reluctant to share true failure numbers with anyone and do not collect numbers if they are bad. Why take the reputational risk, when the marketing machines run so well, and many industry awards go to efforts that ultimately turn out to be functional failures? Case in point: Two years in a row, the application winners of the Windows World Open went on to become legendary disasters. Both of these had required huge investments. When each of these solutions was selected, IT personnel within the respective companies broadly understood these systems to be the legendary failures they would become. "Successes" like these never get accurately classified—in fact, they remain successes because a retraction is never published. Last, every company has a corporate communications function that ensures that whatever is reported by the company paints the right picture.

3. **Beauty is in the eye of the beholder.** Expectations are so low that delivery is often construed as success. Not surprisingly, just completing a project creates a sigh of relief and a bright halo around the development team. Gauging success or failure through this distorted lens causes our industry to understate the magnitude of the problem. Do you think many of today's projects would be classified as a success if expectations were high and success well understood?

   My experience leads me to a simple conclusion: Our collective potential is significantly higher than our results, so our relative success rate is therefore significantly lower than any number reported.

4. **We cannot measure knowledge worker productivity**. The software development industry cannot measure productivity, and every software development project is unique. Consequently, we cannot establish a performance benchmark at the beginning of a project and then compare actual performance to it at the end. So what is a success? Everybody was extremely busy and an end product was created? Very simply, the barometer of success and failure is engineered through expectation management and reporting.

   What remains is the comparative success of one effort versus another. You know the outcome was successful, but you don't know if another group could have done it in half the time or twice the time. The evaluation is totally perceptual.

5. **The opportunity cost of ignoring human potential is colossal**. In terms of unproductive capital, we are conservatively talking in the range of $100 billion dollars. So when speaking of "success," you have to put it in quotes. Unhappiness is a common result, perhaps even an expectation. It is only with great trepidation and uncertainty that a large initiative is funded by a business.

Until the human factors of productivity are understood, embraced, and leveraged, IT will remain a corporate marriage of convenience, driven out of necessity, not love.

If We Would Just Embrace and Trust Our People . . .

The failure rates and dissatisfaction are also brilliantly reflected in the desperate and pathological response by senior management. Time and again, the pressure to fix the "IT performance problem" is answered by an external group of pundits that have a "breakthrough," and time after time, management rushes to embrace this new and wonderful solution. Based on my experience, the internal IT staff always knows when the pundits are wrong, but they are never consulted. Yet this is nothing new, and it's not isolated to IT. It is common to seek "expert" opinion.

There is a compelling book on group intelligence titled *The Wisdom of Crowds* by James Surowiecki.[7] The basic proposition of the book is that a group of well-informed, independent individuals will make a better decision than the best expert operating alone. Surowiecki provides ample proof that this is the case, such as a random group of farmers at a country fair who outperformed a renowned expert by collectively guessing the exact weight of a pig when their answers were averaged. This happened every time they competed—the crowd was wiser. The prevailing wisdom was that the specialist would know better, which highlights how humans find comfort in the opinion of "experts." This must be a feature of the human psyche. Although there is a bias that causes us to "believe in" the expert, in fact each farmer is also an expert, with deep "institutional" experience, gained on the job. This is no different from IT, where each seasoned resource on your internal staff is also an expert. They just aren't treated that way.

Today's overreliance by executive management on external experts breeds social pathology. Am I against experts and using them wisely? Not at all. Companies can benefit from outside expertise, and I am 100 percent for augmenting internal knowledge to stay abreast of changing trends, technologies, and practices. Learning from others is good, and necessary, or your organization risks becoming insular and stale. However, I am also 100 percent for engaging outside experts with your internal experts fully involved, guiding the process, with the final say in how the expertise will be applied. The internal experts are the *only* ones with deep institutional knowledge. You have to trust them, or the outcome is a failure of management, not IT, even though IT is likely to be blamed.

Because technology evolves quickly, it is different from other parts of the corporation. Every few years another silver bullet comes along almost like a wave breaking on the shore. Some generate lasting value and are valuable if used wisely. That said, they are always driven by vendors and are always overhyped.

Each time the bullet is sold to the senior leadership, both IT and non-IT, using a riveting proposition that the solution to fix IT has been found; each time everyone embraces the "easy" way out, even though it appears too good to be true; and each time the answer is found external to management's own experts and staff—*yes, their experts appear better than ours because we only hear what is good about theirs, while we understand what is both good and bad about ours.* Consequently, the trust between management and staff is damaged, as a sense of betrayal pervades the social chemistry.

From what I have experienced, interpersonal trust is a current that flows between individuals. To function fully, the trust must course through the entire social system (up, down, across), an unbroken stream that energizes every human connection. It originates with management and spreads outward from there, but it can also exist between individuals, when management is not trusted. This current gives interpersonal bonds their strength and flows everywhere if connections among individuals and groups are open. If short-circuited, as it is when the trust flows from management to a third party, the basis for success is lost. The weak connections cause the social fabric to fray, and the outcome is disappointing.

Unfortunately, this cycle of hype and failure has been repeated too many times. Table 2.1 highlights some classic silver bullets and how they were over-hyped when they first appeared. Many of these propositions have value—in some cases, great value. The problem is external vendor hype that produces poorly thought-out business decisions as everyone tries to jump on the initial wave.

Table 2.1 shows a few prominent ones.

One of Gartner's standard products is a hype cycle. All new technologies have steep industry learning curves and pioneers always take the arrows. That said, most silver bullets had value if used intelligently. But companies go all in, with executives swinging for home runs, only to find they should have proceeded slowly, trusted their internal experts to figure out how to use the solution correctly, if at all, and then moved ahead. When management does go all in, somewhere along the way victory is declared, and then the truth comes out after they are gone and the damage is done. Broad executive commitments made using 30,000-foot views normally bring tragic results.

Table 2.1   Classic Silver Bullets

Date and Business Proposition	Business Outcome
1980s: *DP Information Engineering* will reduce development time and eliminate programmers. Very expensive but worth it.	Complete failure. Tools like the Information Engineering Workbench (IEW) and Information Engineering Facility (IEF) came with great hype and faded away. Models were not maintained, and new programming languages quickly relegated this method to the junk heap. Duped again.
1990s: *Distributed systems* will replace mainframes, greatly reducing development time and cost.	Didn't come close to the hype at the time. Led to a proliferation of stand-alone databases and solutions that greatly increased the firm's maintenance and development costs, increasing operational risks and data leakage. Distributed was not cheaper, and it increased the cost of doing business as costly security and control challenges permeated corporations. As we head toward "cloud computing," we are basically using a massively parallel "mainframe" in the sky, slowly rolling back to a centralized model.
1990s: *Domestic outsourcing* will allow us to leverage external experts to reduce cost and complexity.	Vendor lock-in is very costly over time, and the external experts are not better than your own. Change orders levered up costs, as complex contracts masked the true cost of this operating model. Often, the outsourced systems were reinternalized at a later date.
1990s: *Enterprise data warehouses* will make the company information rich.	Many IT-driven failures early on. IT-led efforts were not embraced by the business or used only for basic reporting. Some noteworthy successes, but many early enterprise warehouses produced lots of reports and little value.

Table 2.1   Classic Silver Bullets

Date and Business Proposition	Business Outcome
2000s: *Offshoring* is much cheaper, and eventually all software development will migrate to low-cost producers.	Metrics, productivity, and human capital accounting are not understood in IT, so these vital criteria are missing from the business cases. Certainly, dollars per resource hour is not a productivity measure, yet it is the only quantifiable element and therefore is relied on. Offshoring makes development far more complicated and increases the difficulty of innovation. The proper use is for commodity work that has a short time to competency (see Chapter 13), coding a new solution from scratch, or to take advantage of the time differences. This includes nightly production support, legacy maintenance, non–mission-critical systems, some operations functions, and industry standard skills such as server configuration and provisioning.
	Reliance on commodity labor with limited institutional knowledge is slow and unproductive. Companies that have overembraced this proposition will take back critical business functions as the lack of innovation and advancement will lead to competitive disadvantage. Offshoring is a tool that will eventually be used the right way. In the meantime, the damage has been very costly.
1990s and 2000s: A large *ERP* implementation (SAP) will modernize the corporate infrastructure. Goal: Keep up with corporate peers.	The disasters in this space are noteworthy for their frequency of occurrence, negative impact, and private nature. The failures are of the declare-victory-and-move-on variety. Not tracked or admitted to, many are part of IT folklore. Measure twice and cut once.

Some silver bullets, like DP information engineering, are so fundamentally flawed that they are discarded. Others persist, their true potential understood only after much disappointment, at which point they are intimately managed and properly applied. Success is hard to achieve, as it requires finding great talent, embracing it, nurturing it, and figuring out the right answer, which is different for every company. Technology success remains situational and is not one size fits all.

Offshore Outsourcing: A Deeper Look

Let's take a deeper look at offshore IT outsourcing, which is deeply intertwined with the notion of interchangeability of parts. It exploded as the Internet opened up global communications. Clearly, it has very attractive financials when you simplistically compare professionals using hourly rates. But buying professionals by the hour is no different from buying soybeans by the pound. It works only when each bean is the same. However, in IT, the "beans" are vastly different.

Let's compare two resources: an individual with proven high aptitude and 10 years of institutional experience versus an offshore programmer of unknown aptitude, 3 years of programming experience, and no institutional knowledge. Absent productivity metrics, measures of accumulated social capital, and human capital accounting (the acquired value of the on-the-job experience), you end up with a very attractive business case when you compare these individuals by looking at only their cost. But it just isn't true.

It is very expensive to acquire institutional knowledge, because it takes years of hands-on experience to create intimate understanding; it is also very costly to build a high-aptitude team, because years are spent filtering resources to produce a team of bright, socially cohesive professionals, tightly woven into the pulse and fabric of the corporation. In this example, the offshore technician you end up with is most likely average (based on the large numbers entering the profession) and looking for a better opportunity to advance his or her career. (This is normal and expected.) The job hopping produces rapid turnover and loss of institutional experience, which must be then reacquired by a new, average resource. Learning curves are often steep and very costly to climb, but none of this expense is tracked. The lost productivity is enormous. No question about it.

Consequently, in outsourcing deals, the individual knowledge and understanding expensively acquired during years of analysis, debate, and design—the situational knowledge—is accorded zero value. You can slowly comprehend lines of instruction, but the "why" behind each design choice is often lost.

The situational knowledge is the value. Take a system that took 50 person-years to build. At least 25 of those person-years (all of the phases up to construction) represent dollars invested in individuals so they could learn the business and figure out how to automate it—a project is at least half on-the-job education. When these knowledge owners leave, much of that investment goes with them, leaving a series of hard-to-penetrate silos that are partially learned by their successors. The construction process that imparted intimate understanding about the logic, data, architecture, and so on is lost.

As a result, the systems never go away, a costly and permanent reminder of a management decision made based on incomplete understanding. Never mind the destruction of the true source of productivity, a highly cohesive social system that was completely torn asunder as the human resources were swapped. Eventually, you are forced to rewrite the original system, and the corporation re-spends the initial investment trying to relearn the knowledge that is locked in the software. The users are gone because of the automation, and the *knowledge acquirers* are gone as well. The outcome: costly silos where the institutional knowledge has bled away.

We are so driven by short-term thinking. Attractive but untrue financials have created a huge offshoring herd like all other trends, and it hasn't lived up to the hype. Examine what is really happening. IT doesn't work well in most companies, especially those outsourcing/offshoring their talent. You take a discipline that isn't well done and then give this broken function to an offshore provider aligned on maximizing their profit, not yours. As a tool, offshoring only works if you understand the tool, and how to wisely use it given your specific circumstances. Nothing in IT is "one size fits all." Success is always situational.

Moreover, an offshore deal is easy to get into and costly to get out of. If a company succeeds in reinternalizing its systems, it cannot recapture the number of years (pick a large number) of learning that were nonchalantly thrown away in the process—the intimate knowledge a team gains by taking a development effort from concept to reality: the real asset. Now a new fixed cost has been created: the legacy systems that never go away.

It is interesting, and telling, that those of us with deep experience in this business knew that this model had value, but only in specific situations. As Chapter 4 clearly reveals, trying to integrate an offshore, outsourced paradigm into a complex social system that requires deep institutional experience and high aptitude to produce great results is at best a risky proposition. For complex, large-scale work, it is such a barrier that it borders on the foolhardy, as you lose intellectual control of your software, your costs, and your destiny. You just don't know what you've got until it is gone.

Tools must be used wisely. When used the right way, these overhyped silver bullets have added a lot of value. The degree of success is directly tied to the amount of reliance on internal expertise, social collaboration, and experience-building small steps that create proven and realistic business strategies. Deep collaboration across all of IT and the business provides an inclusive dialogue, so the right answer can be collectively managed. Breakthrough propositions have immediate appeal, but the devil is always in the countless details that determine success and failure. Embrace and trust your experts, and rely on them to bring you the truth.

What's the takeaway from all this? Quite simply, relying on big stories and outside experts does not work. IT fails at alarming rates, and employing the "highest-quality" outside ingredients will not inoculate your organization against failure and dissatisfaction.

- Having the best technology doesn't protect you.
- Engaging the most renowned consulting firm doesn't protect you.
- Having the finest processes doesn't protect you.
- Reading every management book doesn't protect you.

- Hiring all MBAs doesn't protect you.
- Having the largest budget doesn't protect you.
- Turning your problem over to an offshore vendor doesn't protect you.
- Embracing Carnegie Mellon's Capability Maturity Model℠ doesn't protect you.
- Having a lot of time doesn't protect you. (It probably will kill you.)

In contrast, what does work is practiced at the leading companies: Google and Apple. They care deeply about acquiring, growing, and retaining top talent; they focus enormous energy on this function and have built cultures where the talent they acquire is proud to become and remain members of the team. Their social environments are conducive to creativity, and they understand that high-aptitude, deeply experienced talent is the only shortcut to competitive advantage. Had they relied on commodity labor to build and design their software (not hardware), they wouldn't be on anyone's radar today. Knowledge workers are an asset, not an expense, and as assets they must be grown. It's that simple.

In the next chapter, we examine how IT failure is rooted in the social pathologies created when we view man as machine, devoid of emotion and feeling, driven by process, disconnected from meaning. By finding the true root cause of failure, we can eliminate it, finally solving this long-standing problem. Now you will see why workers were turned into interchangeable parts.

Notes

1. Frederick P. Brooks Jr. *The Mythical Man-Month* (New York: Addison-Wesley, 1995).
2. The Standish Group, "Chaos," 1995. Available at www.projectsmart.co.uk/docs/chaos-report .pdf.
3. The Standish Group, "Extreme Chaos," 2001.
4. Frank Mattern, "Transforming IT," *McKinsey Quarterly* (December 2002). Emphasis added. Available at www.mckinseyquarterly.com/Transforming_IT_1255.
5. Jamie Guevara, Eric Stegman, and Linda Hall, "IT Key Metrics Data 2011," Key Industry Measures: Insurance Analysis: Multiyear. 2010. Gartner Benchmark Analytics, 2010.
6. Michael Bloch, Sven Blumberg, and Jurgen Laartz, "Delivering Large-Scale IT Projects On Time, On Budget, and On Value," *McKinsey Quarterly* (October 2012).
7. James Surowiecki, *The Wisdom of Crowds* (New York: Anchor, 2005).

CHAPTER 3

Workers as Machines

A Social Pathology

Our predecessors endeavored to make men into machines; we are endeavoring to make machines into men.

—CHARLES EDWARD JERNINGHAM

The uncaring culture that dominates our corporate way of life is deeply rooted in the mechanistic beliefs that formed during the industrial revolution. Our current management ethos evolved in this era, and with it our view of *workers as machines*. This mind-set still governs how we organize and treat our knowledge workers, directing them like unemotional automatons—just parts—versus the thinking, emotional professionals they really are.

During the industrial revolution, machines inspired awe, as they converted raw power into mechanical energy, which turned materials into finished goods. Man was the master; he controlled and directed these deaf and mute slaves, each one dutifully working around the clock if necessary. Acquiring the machines required large capital investments, so management focused on increasing usable output to maximize return on investment, and it succeeded by embracing Taylor's process efficiency (see Chapter 1); the "human resources" were incidental.

He's a Good Hand

Quite to management's liking, the machines were unfeeling and easy to understand. Business now had the ability to break work into discrete steps, yielding an environment that was simple to grasp and manage. Moreover, the human resources were assigned basic tasks that were also easy to comprehend and perform. This followed the ancient practice of dehumanizing work and workers; it was common to refer to laborers as a single body part: the *hand*. You see this in the word *farmhand*; shipmen were called *deckhands*, leading to the phrase "all hands on deck"; if management liked what you did, and you were highly skilled, then you were *a good hand*; and someone of weak moral character was a *loose hand*.

Management needs to simplify things so they are easy to manage. Teaching leaders how to harness organizational emotion and create a positive social climate was never on the radar because it offered no quantifiable return on investment. One hand was as good as another. Today the insensitivity remains, and the feelings, emotions, and relationships that energize collaborative assembly, so critical to information technology (IT) productivity, are unharnessed. Few know how to unlock the emotional and cognitive potential of their workforce. Consequently, the human resources soldier on.

Having passed through many generations of leaders, this mechanistic view is deeply embedded and operates below the level of consciousness—a part of the management psyche, if you will, the suitcase without wheels. This legacy of our industrial heritage is a deep-seated social pathology that pervades our leadership mind-set. By conclusion, human collaborative failure reflects the socially pathological state of our leadership model. Although the failures are almost always blamed on the participants, they are indeed failures by management—make no mistake about it. This belief system is toxic to IT, and has engendered failure since the very beginning of this industry. Management's insensitivity to emotion is the fundamental obstacle, and it remains in our way.

The pathology is real and so is its impact on productivity. Cold, unfeeling environments depress human cognitive output; it is no different from running industrial factories without lubricating the machines. Today's equipment—knowledge workers—slow down when there is no warmth, empathy, or compassion; worse yet, they often find themselves threatened by negative and insensitive behavior. These negative behaviors are toxic—a form of workplace poison; all that matters is how much is ingested. When viewed from the standpoint of productivity, negative behaviors represent a form of friction—*social friction*—that rub workers' emotions the wrong way. Treating workers as interchangeable parts is a destructive belief system, and it always has been.

The Machine Age: Still Felt Today

Over 30 years ago, William Acar and coauthors, from the Wharton School, published an insightful work titled "Bureaucracy as a Social Pathology."[1] This compelling essay reveals how the unemotional, detached management paradigm that we function under today emerged and discusses our inability to change it. This paradigm is not limited to individual companies but is a pathology that has embedded itself so deeply in corporate America that 30 years have elapsed and little has changed. Yes, there are a few young, enlightened companies that serve as beacons in the emotional darkness. But, in classic corporations, the social pathologies are felt most deeply by our knowledge workers, such as those in information technology (IT), who must think, feel, and collaborate to create value.

Bureaucracies emerged in the early nineteenth century and became self-preserving, as can be seen in both government and corporate entities. It is evident that any human institution that persists for a long time becomes self-serving and dysfunctional. I am never surprised to find organizational effectiveness impaired in traditional corporations. This impairment is part of the human condition, as frequently noted in the research papers on the origins of bureaucracy. Consider this definition of bureaucracy: "The maladaptations, the inadequacies, or the dysfunctions which *necessarily* develop within human organizations."[2]

But our view of bureaucracy has evolved from one limited to government to one that considers human social systems (i.e., companies) as well. You don't normally see the word *social* used to refer to a corporation, unless you are talking about a social network of some kind. However, Acar and coauthors use this term in reference to management subsystems.

Applying the concept of social pathology to business, Acar et al. then postulate that "*Social pathology* is the inability or lack of desire in a government/management system to remove a persistent obstruction [e.g., IT failure] to development that *can* be removed, by a change either in the way the system is organized and/or its social or physical environment."[3]

In other words, for "pathology" to exist, the obstruction has to be removable, yet the system is unwilling or unable to do anything about it. This is precisely the situation that corporate America finds itself in today. Despite the repeated failure of technology projects dating back to the beginnings of corporate software development, *the actors change, yet the outcomes remain the same*. We are unable to break free of the pathological social behavior that is embedded within America's bureaucracies. The prevalence of failures across vertical industry groups tells us that this problem exists at the business-sector level and is not isolated to a specific type of company. The broadness of this problem points to our corporate heritage and how this heritage has expressed itself.

According to Acar and coauthors, only two machine age design beliefs are needed to set off the sequence of events that trigger the pathological bureaucracy:

1. "The world is machine-like (deterministic, analysable and predictable; tasks are decomposable into routinizable sub-tasks)."[4]

    Here we see the source of the process methodologies and controls that we have come to rely on. As important as they are, they emanated from the concept of reductionism, a prevalent belief system in the 1800s that enabled Taylor. Our overreliance on processes is problematic because it posits that all things can be broken down into a known set of interdependent steps. *Consequently, it is only the steps that matter.* If a task is not done properly, then, by deduction, the input (labor) for that step must be wrong.

2. "People are machine-like (they can be predicted, motivated by extrinsic rewards and monitored)."[5]

The view that people are machine-like underlies the conclusion that if the right processes are put in place, if the appropriate training is deployed, if the right organizational structure is implemented, and if people are paid for their output, then the factory can be made to run right. Naturally, monitoring and predictability became key governing dimensions of this philosophy, with little to no emphasis placed on understanding the social dimensions of the workplace. Although much has since been written about collaboration, it has not found its way into writings about how to design, lead, or run a social system that is anything but machine-like.

The consequences of our belief system are seen in the work around us. As long as we break down each job into a discrete set of steps and assign appropriately skilled individuals, the job will get done. This single-minded focus on tasks and activities has unintended consequences: Management's emphasis on process—the flowcharts, procedure manuals, approval steps, and so on—has built in the assumption that the right machine (read individual) is of secondary importance. If you don't like the "parts," just get new ones. Therefore, instead of focusing on whether one's people are happy, a leader is more likely to fret over how the process is used.

Philosophically, the industrial bureaucracy had complete faith in man's ability to reduce anything to its most fundamental elements, and these elements in turn could be either automated or staffed with workers. The focus was—and is to this day—on limiting people's ability to think. Process was the beginning and the end. If you fairly examine today's defects/problems in IT, they are often traceable to knowledge workers who have not been encouraged to freely exercise their judgment and bond with their fellow craftsmen. In fact, many have been punished for doing so. Ultimately, the focus is much more on the work processes, not the people doing it.

Frederick Taylor knew that human factors influenced process outcomes in important ways, but he ignored them because they could not be quantified, as required by his efficiency movement. As he noted:

We can see and feel the waste of material things. *Awkward, inefficient, or ill-directed movements of men, however, leave nothing visible or tangible behind them*. Their appreciation calls for an act of memory, an effort of the imagination. And for this reason, even though our daily loss from this source is greater than from our waste of material things, the one has stirred us deeply, while the other has moved us but little.[6]

Taylor believed that improving the efficiency of workers, and of management, was a collective responsibility, so he called for more training. But as founder and leader of the movement, Taylor knew that there were human factors that could be tuned to improve the functioning of business operations. He also knew that there was no science in this area and no way to concretely shape a meaningful measurement and reporting system. As he had no science with which to explore this opportunity, he ignored the human dimensions.

Birth of Corporate Easter Islands

This blind spot remains and has caused IT to fail repeatedly across corporations: It is a long-standing social pathology that emanates from our ignorance of distinctly human factors—multiple intelligences, emotions, and the social systems that underlie the collaborative creation of software-based products and services. Our view is so industrial—machines, process, output, measurement—that the ultimate drivers of social success, and human potential, are not seen, tracked, managed, or talked about. We blindly ignore the human factors of success as if it were possible to *process manage* a group of artists and derive a great, predictable outcome. It isn't going to happen.

As a result of viewing workers as machines, our workforce has become stone-faced and devoid of emotion, similar to the statues in Figure 3.1. At a time when we must breathe creative life into our organizations, many companies seem more like Easter Island.

Our Human Resource Practices Remain Primitive

Our reliance on process instead of people has cultivated a very uncaring, selfish work environment that treats staff members like expendable commodities instead of integral pieces of the creative and collaborative social fabric.

These Easter Islands are multibillion-dollar laboratories where cold, disconnected leadership styles are the norm and where mega-project failures and the human root causes are never adequately documented or understood. Our machine-age view of workers disregards the people and their movements, so the lessons learned from project failures often result in a simple edict: Collaboration needs to improve. It seems almost as if mentioning the fact is an adequate

Figure 3.1 Easter Island: The Beatings Won't Stop until Morale Improves (Clichés Reflect Deeply Held Beliefs)
Source: Image credit: www.123rf.com/photo_9618910_faces-of-four-stone-moai-in-easter-island-on-sunny-day.html.

prescription. In reality, this is a gross oversimplification caused by our blindness to the human factors that underpin meaningful collaboration. What ultimately governs success is how tightly bound and resilient the social fabric is across business and IT. Everything else is secondary. Our attempt to manage and lead people-centric activities with an industrial-era bias is also felt in the coldness of the term *human resources*. Unconsciously, we embrace the view that people are, after all, just resources like electricity, machines, supplies, parts, manuals, inventory—the building blocks of a prior age. Notions like this are part of our management subconscious, the inherited DNA that individuals acquire as they are reared in the corporate world. As they learn and mature, they acquire a belief system that has been passed between generations of managers.

Hiring remains more primitive than it should be. Many times I've seen "parts" ordered by engaging a recruiter who goes online and matches the "parts list" against the Internet (the parts inventory). Professionals resort to gaming the system by investing time to fill their resume with the right search terms, so they become a hit. It goes something like this:

I need to place an order for two dozen humans. Please mark this order rush, because I need the parts in inventory by next Friday. My requirement is that each human comes with 16 years of education, the skills listed on the attached specification, and an ability to communicate. Make sure you check off the items on the attached list, because I need an exact match. Precision matters.

If an individual challenges these heritage notions, he or she will fail, because the prevailing wisdom is so deeply held that the *bureaucracy cannot change itself from within.* The lone voice calling out from inside the walls of the corporation will never be heard.

Transforming the corporate sector requires a broad social movement that evolves our understanding from the outside in, as witnessed in the early 1900s when Taylorism set the stage for the continuous process improvement paradigm passed down to us today.

Selectively Continue the Past; Fully Embrace the Future

We are still in the infancy of the information era. As in the early part of the industrial era, today's workers are closer to craftspeople who leverage professional skill to turn out custom parts. Groups of these craftspeople are united to create *social systems* where a prescribed set of steps is followed to create a product. No two runs of this modern assembly line are ever the same, and each output is unique. The process is both sequential and highly parallel at the same time, requiring many groups working alongside one another— multiple lines, if you will—that ultimately meet to construct the end product. Unlike the industrial age, however, we have not achieved a quantum leap in productivity and repeatability.

That era endowed us with many techniques that built a strong foundation for us—processes, controls, quality management, and so on. However, the process centricity failed to recognize what drives the human machines that are now the source of value creation. In this regard, we must embrace the learnings of the industrial era while rejecting the selfish and inhumane management practices that led to unionization. Had management embraced the employees, worked with them, and leveraged their knowledge to collectively advance their companies, the results would have been richer and longer lasting. We see that the unionized models had baked in the seeds of their own destruction, a bias toward selfishness versus productivity, and the remnants of that era persist in weak (U.S. automobile) or protected (teachers, municipal workers) environments. This adversarial model is highly unproductive and selfish in its own right, but it is the natural reaction to very shortsighted treatment.

Knowledge workers are treated as equipment in traditional corporate America, but without any monitoring, operator's manuals, and so on. If the

United States is to dominate the twenty-first-century global information economy, then we must not allow our industrial roots to corrode the rise of prosocial environments where harmony, empathy, compassion, and deep institutional experience are valued as productive. If we do, it will consume both our wealth and our economic potential while opening the door for a more sensitive and forward-looking competitor to take the leadership mantle away from us. We must nurture a productive, mutually respectful relationship, built on the notion that a strong, supportive embrace produces richer results than the cold, machinelike bond that overhangs the industrial age.

So the prescription is this: Socially intelligent managers who use trust and sensitivity as a flowing current to productively connect groups of knowledge workers will no longer manage the human infrastructure, but will artfully unlock their employees' full potential.

Individually, we are one drop. Together, we are an ocean.

—Ryunosuke Satoro

But we aren't there yet. One of the pathologies created by viewing man as machine is that the machines don't matter, enabling an environment where selfishness can flourish and be justified. It is the root cause of IT failure. In Chapter 5, we look at a case study that lays out how just such an environment created conditions *toxic to productivity*. The financial impact of these social pathologies is enormous, and very clear. But first, let's look at how IT is a creative endeavor requiring many minds and emotions so that the pathological impact of antisocial behavior is clear when you get there.

Notes

1. William Acar, Jahangir Pourdehnad, Paramjit S. Sachdeva, and Sanjay Sharan, "Bureaucracy as a Social Pathology," Social Systems Sciences Department, University of Pennsylvania, 1981. Available at http://knowledge.wharton.upenn.edu/papers/555.pdf.
2. Ibid., 2, quoting from M. Crozier, *The Bureaucratic Phenomenon* (Chicago: University of Chicago Press, 1964). Emphasis in original.
3. Ibid., 8.
4. Ibid.
5. Ibid.
6. Frederick W. Taylor, *The Principles of Scientific Management*. Modern History Sourcebook. Emphasis added. Available at www.fordham.edu/halsall/mod/1911taylor.html.

CHAPTER 4

The Unseen Art and Emotion of IT

The Acme Inc. Philharmonic Orchestra: Knowledge as Notes, Leaders as Conductors, Programmers as Composers

Growing up human is uniquely a matter of social relations rather than biology. What we learn from connections within the family takes the place of instincts that program the behavior of animals; which raises the question, how good are these connections?

—ELIZABETH JANEWAY

To create a software-based product, groups of knowledge workers are assigned the task of creating a solution. The construction process requires information technology (IT) and business professionals to collaborate deeply, exchanging thoughts and ideas until a shared understanding of the desired product emerges. Although they have common goals, each group of professionals sees, feels, and experiences the project using their different innate intelligences. Consequently, they speak about the same things but perceive them differently.

The business is on the outside looking in. These professionals see presentations, participate in meetings, review plans, and read documents; they touch the product development process through the physical reality of charts, words, and language. But the technology professionals cross over this physical boundary into the realm of the conceptual. They marry creativity with abstraction and conceptualization to translate this physical world into a technical design; they rely on flashes of creativity, strong visualization skills, and experience that is broadly distributed across team members; finally, they rely on positive emotions and strong human connections to draw out group intelligence as they shift from concept to reality. It is a cast of highly skilled specialists who turn ideas into working products, who operate in a conceptual reality that cannot be seen, and who are codependent on one another for success. It is this unseen realm of mind and emotion that governs success and failure.

This chapter exposes the unseen by using a musical metaphor to reveal the hidden aspects of this conceptual and emotional reality. Within IT, we see the evolution from *process-based efficiency*, the breakthrough of the industrial era, to *people-based potential*, the revolution of an emerging socioproductive age. The social system is the factory.

A Product of Mind and Emotion

Looking in on a project from the outside, one sees a group of IT professionals who spend their days in meetings; interpret and document the results of those meetings (often inaccurately if you ask the business); prepare PowerPoint presentations to communicate representations of what they are building; use too many acronyms; overcomplicate simple goals; take too long to deliver anything; spend far too much money; estimate their work very poorly; rely on strange and often incommunicative workers; and ultimately appear less than expert at what they do.

Although technology-based products and services form the heart of many businesses, those external to the discipline poorly understand the IT profession and its value creation process—individual projects and highly complex programs that combine multiple projects into streams of work. The highly evolved art form used to build technology solutions (a combination of software and hardware) still remains largely a black box to those who are not in this profession.

The business leaders and partners who rely on IT projects, as well as many workers within the profession itself, can neither see nor feel the inner reality of the solutions development processes. Definitively, the most important element of IT—the professional—is often consigned to an organization chart and a headcount planning listing. As a legacy of our manufacturing heritage, they are merely accounting entries in budget spreadsheets (i.e., human resources). If you take attendance and they are present, then all is good.

Our business leaders, unable to see the inner workings of a project, are forced to rely instead on manufacturing-era process representations, construction plans, resource and capital budgets, narrative descriptions of technologies, and architecture diagrams. Although all of these are important communication and control instruments, they nevertheless neuter an inherently social endeavor and leave the cognitive and social levers of productivity deeply masked underneath words, flows, and numbers. Here success is deeply dependent on cross-disciplinary teams of highly trained co-creators. The creativity, the emotion, the technical skill, the personal interaction, the human desire—the true essence of the development process and the ultimate success drivers—are not modeled, monitored, valued, or controlled.

So we have injected all of our industrial-era biases and knowledge to make an inherently emotional, artistic endeavor conform to our notion of industrial control and engineering. At their core, IT projects are far more creative and conceptual than they are process based. Not to say that process is not extremely important. The lessons from the industrial age must not be lost and should be embraced for what they are: valuable building blocks upon which we will erect a productive social structure rooted in human understanding.

These building blocks are depicted below in the bottom half of Figure 4.1 and represent the process-based efficiency Taylorism launched at the beginning of the twentieth century. The social levers of production—the essence of collaborative knowledge work—exist above the industrial-era competencies of *process management* and *control*. These new layers, *the human factors*, are the information economy's foundation for efficiency, and in IT they are expressed within supportive social environments—or not, which produces failure. What we are experiencing in this transition between eras is tumultuousness, as the old system recedes into the background and human understanding comes to the foreground.

Excitingly, we have front-row seats to watch the evolution of the corporation. The industrial species has evolved into two organisms that operate

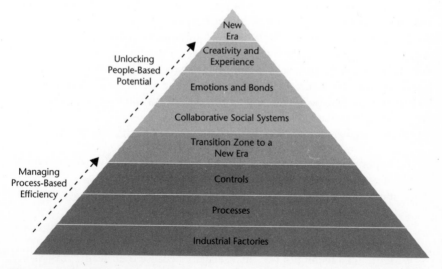

Figure 4.1 Transition between Eras

alongside one another: the postindustrial corporation (e.g., Apple and Google) versus more traditional ones (e.g., General Motors). This is not unlike the evolution of humankind where Neanderthals were found to have lived alongside early modern humans, only to disappear because they were less well adapted. Google, of course, is far more collaborative and has prevailed, as Darwin pointed out:

> In the long history of humankind (and animal kind, too) those who learned to collaborate and improvise most effectively have prevailed.

So the evolution takes time as we move from a dependence on process to one dependent on people. Process remains our foundational heritage—still very important but no longer the focus. The process-based model perfected over the last century has served the economy very well, creating great wealth and excellent returns on capital. Unquestionably, process was good, is good, and will remain very good. As a result, *software engineering* fully leveraged process knowledge to introduce order and discipline through the use of solutions development methodologies, program management, quality assurance, and the like.

Dividends have been realized, but our sole reliance on process has had a debilitating impact. It cannot take advantage of human potential and the highly varied aptitudes and emotional intelligences of professionals. These differences are the source of the great productivity variances Frederick Brooks referred to as the mythical man-month—simply put, no two people are equally competent and equally experienced. There is no such thing as a person-month of work.

Beyond this, as knowledge workers are assigned to a project, a social system forms that requires meaningful human interaction to unleash productive value. Each social system is a unique milieu—an environment—that supports or constrains the creation of this value. It is within this milieu that thought, conceptualization, emotion, behavior, caring, and relationships blend together to shape the performance of the workers. This endeavor is human and highly emotional, passing through peaks and valleys of feelings as the project progresses.

If the social chemistry among team members is healthy, they may:

- Experience rushes of excitement as they creatively solve complex technical challenges.
- Feel happy and content once they recognize how cohesive and talented their team is.
- Form deep personal relationships with co-creators who selflessly share their knowledge and insight.
- Develop a feeling of personal security because their leader unselfishly watches their back instead of his or her own.

- Overcome complex creative challenges by drawing on the confidence of a supportive group and their prior achievements.
- Feel joy as co-creators show appreciation for each other's contributions.
- Form lifetime friendships by overcoming adversity with the help of others.
- Become resilient as they master unfamiliar and complex tools.
- Share admiration for one another.
- Feel great satisfaction as they unravel a complex technical puzzle.
- Struggle to understand their role within the overarching plot.
- Develop great appreciation for coworkers who selflessly share their knowledge, insight, and time in spite of personal deadlines that are very challenging.
- Appreciate brilliance as almost incomprehensible technical challenges are adeptly mastered by a team member.
- Laugh as humor erupts to counterbalance the stress and failures.

However, if they are in a corrosive social environment, they are likely to:

- Ignore the derogatory comments of a corrosive leader by tapping self-esteem to remain intrinsically motivated.
- Witness intrigue as professionals selfishly conspire to twist technology decisions in a direction closely aligned with their expertise and therefore personal security.
- Suffer embarrassment as carefully thought-out decisions become public disappointments.
- Endure waves of adrenaline and stress as their team struggles to meet mandated and unachievable deadlines.
- Feel satisfaction as they unravel the hidden agendas they felt were there but had been cleverly disguised.
- Suppress waves of anger as an incompetent peer is recognized by a "leader" who never worked in the profession and is unable to discern fact from fiction.
- Confront fear as they run into unexpected hurdles because communication and collaboration were inadequate.
- Encounter deception at the hands of incompetent yet codependent peers.
- Sense desperation in a co-creator assigned deliverables beyond their capability and experience, yet never reach out to help because they might be blamed if the individual fails in spite of their assistance.
- Feel anger as unreliable coworkers make commitments and fail to meet them.

- Endure betrayal at the hands of management who, as nonpractitioners, make uninformed decisions that set a *Titanic* project on a collision course with failure.

If you have moved across companies, you have most likely seen and felt supportive and destructive social environments. One unlocks human potential; the other destroys it. Building a complex, *n*-tiered (many different layers of technology) system involving hundreds of specialists is one of the most complex undertakings in modern business. Because of that, these two subplots are normally operating together, with swings of emotion as the effort progresses. It is usually not a case of one or the other.

The set of emotions and behaviors produced by healthy and unhealthy social environments are completely different: one highly productive, the other highly corrosive. Normally, I arrive when toxic behaviors have led to undeniable failure. The truth, known to many from early in the project life cycle, finally shines through the fog of disinformation and the need for a leadership change becomes self-evident. That is how toxicity ends.

Limitations of Language and Our Resultant Inability to Communicate

As an industry, IT has failed to train the business so they can understand how our engineers and artists accomplish what they do. If this type of clarity were imparted to those looking in, they would grasp the nuance and challenges that often cause large projects to fail and would be able to infer the impact of their decisions on the course of a large development effort. But could they also grasp the underlying potential?

Simply put, today's business/IT union is a mature relationship in which neither love nor intimacy has been achieved. It is like a poor marriage, where the partners are staying together for the sake of the family—I can't live with you, and I can't live without you. Although divorce has been tried many times—outsourcing, offshoring, and so on—this marriage is still active, only strained even further by outside experts who counsel that the marriage must be dissolved because others are more compatible. At this point a healthy bond must be formed, one based on harmony and understanding, not distrust and misunderstanding.

The root cause of this marital breakdown is ineffective communication, misunderstanding, and the overarching feeling of incompatibility this has bred. After living together for so many years, the business still does not understand its IT spouse. Although they work together, much of what the spouse does remains shrouded in mystery. Unbeknownst to the business, the spouse is an artist who works in the corporate orchestra with eccentric composers who collaborate in the creation of complex works.

The orchestra, you say? Yes. While building IT organizations, companies have acquired large groups of creative performers who join together in what abstractly resembles a *business orchestra*. These orchestras are composed of individuals that compose works (solutions), have deep expertise in a large variety of instruments (programming and design tools), need conductors to guide them (in the creation process), never duplicate existing compositions (every work is unique), create harmony out of many individual contributions (like the players in an orchestra), practice frequently (or lose their touch), create best when in tune with one another (they jam), and can see the "work" that will ultimately be created (although not notes on a score).

Most surprisingly, you don't lead or manage these workers; you *conduct* them. With an emotionally charged baton, the conductor connects with the unseen social levers of production to craft beautiful, collaboratively created compositions that run our modern corporations.

The industrial enterprise, our source of the notion of management, was formed to guide industrial assembly processes and fine-tune the manufacture of physical products. This form of production is vastly different from the collaborative assembly process today's knowledge workers employ to deliver a great performance. Although "assembly" is required, the output is *intellectual property*, not physical goods; the creation process is talent-centric, not robotic; and the hottest products come when those doing the assembly really care about their work and feel someone cares about them. That requires a servant conductor who loves the orchestra and leads it from the heart.

The human machine comes equipped with *thoughts, feelings, intuition, and sensations*. These four aspects of personality that Carl Jung made clear so long ago in his book *Psychological Types* and Katharine Cook Briggs and her daughter, Isabel Briggs Myers, brought into mainstream business, are complex tools that must be harnessed to engender human collaborative progress.[1] Try to *process manage* these machines, as we do today, and you will always get unpredictable results. Try to understand them and design work according to who and what they are, and your outcomes turn positive. That is why the human factors of productivity, like the professionals, cry out to be recognized.

These artists not only think, they feel. The broader skills that humans possess need to be used to enliven the complex interactions that determine whether the behavior is socioproductive. Ignore this, and, like a rudderless ship, you will be tossed about by the waves of emotion and carried to a destination of the current's choice. The project is lost at sea.

The orchestras also come in many sizes: Some are small chamber ensembles, while others are very large, composed of many smaller ones. Conductors who know how to lead a small group of musicians lead the chamber orchestras, and a master conductor who knows how to lead both musicians and conductors ultimately leads the overall symphony.

So, at a genuine level, there is a very concrete overlap between two unique artistic professions. The intersection looks something like the comparison in Figure 4.2.

Social Cohesion and Conceptual Unity

The key output of the orchestra is a usable solution, an end product that is the equivalent of a symphonic score in music that is ready to be performed. But there is one critical difference that makes crafting a technology work magnitudes more complicated for these artists than for an individual composer. The music composer scores the symphony alone—a single creative mind, a clear goal, inspiration, personal desire, and lots of hard work. This is then performed by a symphony orchestra. The entire *business orchestra*, in contrast, composes its work using software development instruments and tools. This is group composition, an inherently social endeavor captured in the phrase *out of many minds, one*. As captured by the motto of the United States, *E pluribus unum* ("out of many, one"), individual (state) and group (federal) needs have

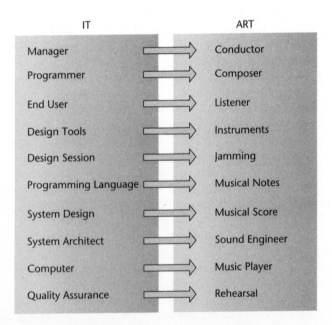

Figure 4.2 Creative Roles Masked by Traditional Job Titles

to be balanced in order to craft a productive union, which is precisely why I prefer a federated organizational design (see Chapter 14).

Within this union, each member of the orchestra provides part of the score: notes, phrases, or an arrangement (architecture), all composed according to the "sound" the user has described. This orchestra is collaborative and will fail to produce anything if meaningful social collaboration is not alive. So this social system does not play music; its members collaborate to compose the music. Truly, out of many minds, you end up with one set of thoughts; a concerted effort, by tens or hundreds of brains, each contributing pieces of the ultimate score (solution), based on their specific expertise.

Further complicating this challenge, the individuals asking for the composition do not play music. They cannot speak with you, musician to musician; they cannot directly contribute a set of notes; they can only describe the sounds (with great difficulty), which requires that everything must be translated and all of the holes must be filled in by the composers; they cannot participate in the discussions that the composers have among themselves, where the real creative activity occurs; they ultimately contribute ideas and concepts that have to be internalized and translated from words into IT reality. So it's not surprising when the composers and business folks say they are totally aligned, that the business doesn't like the melody when the final work is played for them. Therefore the cliché: "Business users know what they want when they see [hear] it."

Here you have an orchestra whose members employ their highly specialized skills to collaboratively write a unique "symphony" for their business partners. The longer the piece—that is, the more complex the project—the more likely some users are not going to like the outcome. This is understandable, for as the orchestra grows in size to meet the demand, the risk of disharmony developing increases. If the social environment is toxic, then disharmony is guaranteed.

There are other risks caused by size. When the challenge grows too complex, the work suffers because the buyer (the business) grows impatient with how long the composition is taking, sometimes even canceling the effort; if it is delivered, very likely the final work won't be a thing of beauty.

It also takes a highly visual conductor to sensitively guide a large social system along a creative path and create a shared understanding of the entire work; a high degree of collaboration and communication is needed to ensure that each composer grasps how his or her piece fits into the whole so that the collective product sounds sweet and unified. Overcoming all of the social resistance is a major challenge, especially in the insensitive social environment that characterizes American business. This is one reason big projects fail at higher rates.

Yet it is in a symphonic composition like this that two interdependent and incompatible worlds meet. Below the *transition zone*, we have leaders and workers steeped in industrial-era practices who must rely on a social system of professionals that speaks using foreign terms and concepts. The business partners ultimately rely on these "musical works" to run their business, though they are not required to learn music or understand what makes an orchestra productive; they are uninformed buyers.

This lack of understanding is one of the great opportunities in traditional corporate America. Like finance, budgets, planning, marketing, and domain-specific areas of business expertise, business users should also be required to have basic expertise in IT if their positions depend on it—no ifs, ands, or buts. Enough already! Professionals need cross-domain knowledge when it is an important aspect of their jobs—and that should include IT.

As the percentage of automated business processes continues to increase, the situation may soon take care of itself. That percentage is now at a level where the functions could even be merged. The artificial boundary between IT and the business—"We own the automated piece of the process and you own the unautomated part"—makes no sense and has been the source of many disconnects. The leaders in both areas need all the required expertise.

Now, referring back to Figure 4.1, you will see that it has two distinct layers: one that is process-based and one that is people-based. Here we transition from the *tangible* (touch it, read it) to the *conceptual/emotional* (imagine it, feel it).

In a business setting, everyone within the corporation can understand the process (tangible) layer. This is a familiar, comfortable level, one where common terms and well-understood concepts provide a shared basis for discussion and understanding. Each element in this layer originated in the industrial era and is something you can touch—a document, a presentation, a spreadsheet, a process flow, a control report, a business model. It exists as it is and is what it is.

This is the domain of the business that evolved over the last 200 years. Here you find the financial controls, communication methodologies, process definitions, management reporting, product definitions, and critical objectives. Here you also find disciplines like process management, cost accounting, quality control, marketing communications, financial control, progress reporting, and the like. Each is tangible, physical, and very real—the materials of standard business. This area is well understood. It is what it is and is not an abstraction of itself. Most important, value creation no longer takes place in this area—it is reported and managed here, but little is invented.

The conceptual layer, however, is interpreted by words like *grasp*, *see*, *get*, *comprehend*, *sense*, and *feel*, and is shared through debate and discussion over the value of abstract concepts that are imagined and conceived. When the conceptual layer is built, it is physically streams of bits and bytes that course over layers of communication networks, translated by different presentation devices that allow us to interact with these streams in a variety of ways.

What is conceptualized is an abstract representation of this very different reality. All of the industrial minds grab onto the presentation layer (user interface) and elevate its importance because it is what they see and grasp—their portal into the digital world underneath. Yet great genius concealed inside the system architecture and application design creates cost-effective, flexible, brilliant solutions. This abstraction requires real professional skill to create and cannot be experienced unless you are inside the creation and comprehension process. Otherwise, it is a black box.

Because of our industrial biases, the physical domain is accorded all of the importance. Consequently, on any given project, documents are the deliverables—the manufacturing outputs, if you will. Following the logic of process management, development progress is tracked, and if a document is delivered on time, "the project is progressing as required." You get a gold star. But this emphasis is totally misplaced; the physical biases of the industrial era continue to blind us to the conceptual reality.

Take a *business requirements* document. Although this specification is captured in writing and delivered, the document is actually the by-product, not the deliverable. The actual deliverable is the learning and understanding internalized by a diverse group of minds that must share a conceptual view of the desired solution. If they don't, watch out—the fact that the document is well prepared will quickly be shown to be irrelevant.

The debate, the social collaboration, the give-and-take, the openness to new ideas, the involvement of all the required minds—this is what gradually imparts knowledge, insight, and enlightenment so the composers fully absorb and connect all the dots of the product definition. What ultimately exists in each of the composers' minds is what matters, as it is in the gray matter, not the paper, through which the rest of the project will be realized. The complex, interactive process of learning through sharing is the deliverable, and if that does not go well and the right minds do not acquire what they need, the physical document will falsely signal things are okay. Eventually the project train will derail, and then everyone will ask how this could happen, when "everything was flawlessly on track. Look at the quality of the documentation."

TIP

Requirements definition is not a book but a learning process.

This learning process is complex and very costly. It consumes a lot of time and money. Clearly, the larger the composition, the greater the number of pieces it contains. Larger compositions necessitate enlarging the orchestra, because each piece must be individually crafted and then knitted together across many different minds that hear and interpret differently. The knowledge acquisition process requires a combination of learning new concepts, combining these concepts to form a mental picture, and translating the picture into a physical document or model that can be discussed.

If you are working on a composition that will take 100 person-years to develop, you will spend the first 50 understanding and defining the composition that has been ordered. So although a highly abstract and conceptual conductor can envision the big picture very quickly, the individual pieces take a very long time to model and build. The underlying learning and understanding continues until the very end, when testing helps identify not only errors but also misinterpretations and misunderstandings. As the composers correct these, they finally perfect their understanding. The learning process is now complete.

TIP

The quality of solution is a direct reflection of the cohesiveness of the social system that delivered it.

And the Instruments Keep Changing

Another factor that makes this orchestra so much different is instruments that evolve and change rapidly. Unlike a musical orchestra where they are static, IT instruments come and go, and some stay around much longer than they should. In such cases, it is very difficult even to find someone who plays this outdated, now "obscure" instrument; moreover, no one new wants to learn it, because it has limited value (like studying Latin). The fact that new instruments must be mastered, while few die away, adds greatly to the complexity of running IT over time.

Although the rate of change varies based on whether IT is in a growth cycle (distributed computing, the Internet, etc.) or a digestion cycle (waiting for the next wave to arrive), IT is always changing. That means you are continually adding musicians to the orchestra or training some existing artists to play the new instruments. This organic change and growth makes composing works that much more difficult. Not only do you have to deal with the baseline complexity of the business and size of the project; you also have to accept a certain amount of growth in that complexity, or else you fall behind the market. Ultimately, new technologies are turned into great business models, so you will be playing catch-up if you are not internalizing these changes as they arrive.

The Encore. A Callback. Bravo!

One of the great accomplishments for the orchestra, especially for the conductor, is to be called back for an encore. The bravos mean you have successfully overcome the language barrier, the difficulty of creating a common understanding across many minds, the social ineptitude that exists on Easter Island, and a genuine lack of appreciation for some of the best talent because their value cannot be seen by non-musicians. The need to commit to the cost of creating the requested symphony up front, even though over half of the work is figuring out just what it is, adds to the stress and the challenge of composing a great work.

These factors, among others, lead to the high failure rates projects experience today. Those that overcome these obstacles deserve major kudos. Some failures can be traced to lack of defined processes, but the primary cause is selfish and antisocial behavior that destroys the social fabric, disrupting the network over which communication flows, destroying meaning, causing protective and unproductive behaviors, and zapping the emotional energy that drives success. Chapter 5 examines a project where antisocial behavior became dominant following real success. It shows just how much damage an antisocial leader can create.

Note

1. Carl Jung wrote *Psychological Types* in 1921. I read the book years ago and found it very heavy, although it is important because it is the basis of the Myers-Briggs Type Indicator. Jung was incredibly insightful and ahead of his time, identifying two judging styles (Thinking and Feeling) and two perception styles (Sensation and Intuition). In the patients he worked with, he also observed that each of these styles could be either introverted or extroverted. Therefore, he came up with eight personality types.
   Myers and Myers Briggs used Jung's work to build a tool that is heavily used in mainstream business today. The Myers-Briggs Type Indicator (MBTI) is used to determine people's preferred psychological processes for making decisions and interpreting the world. The mother/daughter duo built a model that used Jung's eight types, and added two dimensions, Judging and Perception, so there are 16 types in their framework.

CHAPTER 5

Case Study: An Unproductive State of Mind

Toxic Leadership and Its Aftermath

Teamwork is the ability to work together toward a common vision. The ability to direct individual accomplishments toward organizational objectives. It is the fuel that allows common people to attain uncommon results.

—ANDREW CARNEGIE

Information technology (IT) is inherently about working social. Our poor results reflect how our weak understanding of the human infrastructure impedes the complex human collaboration that underpins the information economy's growth and highlights corporate America's inability to reliably lead large teams of knowledge workers to greatness. Our collective blindness to distinctly human factors like emotion and social intelligence reveals itself in the ongoing struggle between our desires and our outcomes. This current state of corporate IT cries out for a human solution rather than another silver bullet. We must embrace our professionals or continue to accept low returns on human capital.

The machines are human, the primary tools are brains, and the interconnections are emotional bonds that tie the "machines" in the assembly network together. IT performs best when the contributors work in a socially cohesive, nurturing environment. When they don't, the results are disastrous, as clearly seen in the following case study.

An Unproductive State of Mind

The Study

Socially Toxic Leadership. How a manager's behavior destroyed a high performing team, more than doubling a project's cost. The names have been changed to protect the guilty.

The Challenge

In IT, it is difficult to find a case study that enables you to quantify the impact of a manager who creates a social environment that is toxic to productivity. Software development, unlike manufacturing, produces custom products. Projects, products, and teams vary, with no two exactly alike, so it is difficult to attribute an overrun to a clear root cause. Manufacturing is the opposite. You manufacture a product—in fact, a lot of them. Each time you run the assembly line, you have a specific number of identical outputs and a total cost. By simply dividing the total cost by the number of units, you arrive at a unit cost. Because you know the unit cost, you can identify the productivity impact of process changes, organizational changes, or changes to the product design, as the cost per unit moves up and down. But IT is custom work, so you are often comparing apples and oranges. No two projects are identical. However, after speaking with many people, I did find the perfect case study, the needle in the haystack. If this were a Hollywood movie, it would be an action film, where an unsuspecting group of actors suddenly find their safe, happy, and socially cohesive environment is becoming a threatening, dangerous, and toxic nightmare. Enjoy the show!

The Interview

For this case study, I interviewed Robert Iannone, who spent many years in consulting, including a stint during which he owned his own firm. At the time of this interview, he was at a midsize consulting firm, in charge of its solutions practice. This is what he witnessed.

The Setting

Act I of our drama begins with a consulting engagement at AnyCompany, Inc., a Fortune 500 company. The IT division at AnyCompany had no spare capacity, but the business had been strenuously pushing to add automated workflow to 15 distinct business processes. As an accommodation, the IT area engaged Robert's consulting firm to work directly with its business partners. This project became an ideal case study because the *current state assessment* identified 15 process automation projects, each nearly equal in scope.

That said, the first project was the largest because it included building the technical foundation the next 14 workflow projects would use; it was completed on time, over a period of four months, for $460,000. The business loved the outcome.

But the honeymoon was already over. Act II would prove completely different. The IT organization inserted itself and put its manager in charge. The second iteration, scoped at 70 percent of the work effort (no foundation), cost double. Here's what happened.

The Root Cause

IT is a product of many minds and emotions, woven into a team, tasked with co-creating a solution. In this case, the technical team comprised a dozen individuals that included a project manager, four business analysts, six net programmers, and one quality assurance analyst. They were embedded in the business, and although they hadn't worked together before, the team gelled quickly and built a strong rapport with the business team.

For the first release, the social environment was healthy, characterized by prosocial behaviors like sharing, inclusiveness, and respect for one another; it was led by an empathetic and caring manager who was competent and had the team's back and the best interest of the business in mind. The walls came down quickly, replaced by bridges; there was almost no politics, plenty of deep and meaningful collaboration, and frequent, open communication; it was an environment where everyone was encouraged to speak up.

Since the business fought for extra help and got it, there was genuine joint ownership and a warm, healthy relationship between them and the consulting team. The consultant project manager showed how he cared by checking to make sure all team members had what they needed and showed appreciation for the effort they put in—so they worked hard. The team used frequent, deeply collaborative meetings to ensure everyone heard the same information and maintained a flat structure with no hierarchy, creating an environment where everyone was equal. They built a release of working code every two weeks, creating a sense of accomplishment, and cycled through frequent builds, producing a well-designed, high-quality product in four months. The business loved the outcome.

This was a great example of a social environment conducive to knowledge worker productivity. In a healthy social climate, the technicians feel safe and relaxed. Their minds are free to focus on the task at hand, allowing creativity to flow and trusting relationships to form; with an empathetic and caring manager, the team's productivity rose, as was demonstrated by the Hawthorne Western Electric studies back in the 1920s (see Chapter 6); the team was socially cohesive, so they joked around with one another, unlocking creativity, an effect also scientifically proven; last, when a team is greeted with enthusiasm, warmth, and high expectations, as was the case here, performance rises to meet those same expectations, an effect Robert Rosenthal demonstrated in a double blind study (see Chapter 6). Harmony drives productivity; when you have harmony and prosocial leadership, you have a powerful emotional foundation on which to build success.

But it wasn't meant to be. This IT area didn't have a good relationship with the business, and its track record wasn't positive. Observing from a distance, the internal IT manager had become resentful of the consulting team's success so, for the second project, this individual assigned an AnyCompany project manager and took back control. The mood darkened quickly; the new manager immediately found fault with the team structure and broke it apart, assigning two new business analysts a time zone away, and moved the quality assurance role offshore; the consultant project manager was sidelined as part of the power play, stripped of control but left dangling. Consulting team members were told they couldn't talk with anyone, and an "interpreter" was put between them and their former coworkers in the business.

Counterproductive and antisocial behavior replaced teamwork and harmony. Blame, ostracism (the consulting project manager was ostracized), deceit, hidden agendas, threats, insincerity, intimidation, conflict, public embarrassment, and emotional aggression were all part of the mix. People, afraid to speak up, shut down instead.

The new manager, driven by insecurity and the resentment that breeds, began to berate the deliverables, leading daily conference calls that were negative, adversarial, blame oriented, and degrading. Two of the original team members left—the lucky ones, in retrospect, given that the beatings continued—and the stress continued to rise. As productivity dropped, overtime skyrocketed but the consultants remained professional and worked harder to keep the project on track. The first project, which was challenging, now felt effortless in comparison to this environment, which was highly toxic to productivity. A strongly cohesive team had been quickly shattered.

Work began to slip, but the internal project manager who had been assigned also feared the boss's selfish and antisocial behavior. It wasn't just the external consultants who were being bullied; the behavior was meted out to all subordinates. It was a classic case of *kiss up and kick down*. The project manager reported that everything was on time, playing *extend and pretend*, rather than face the emotional outburst the truth would unleash. The senior management had no visibility into this social environment, so the corrosive leader operated with impunity. Although it didn't come out in the interview, destructive leaders like this always seek out those who speak the truth and force them out of the organization, creating zombies out of those who remain: devoid of joy, going through the motions, emotionally depressed, cleverly protecting themselves, but soldiering on to earn a living.

As extensively covered already, IT is a product of mind and emotion. Unlike a factory, where it is obvious if the assembly line slows, all creative work is occurring internally, in the brain. It is only visible to those with the right Emotional Quotient (EQ).[1] You have to tune into your organization using social intelligence to interpret the productivity vibe seen through each professional's expressions; only then do you know if *their factory of the mind* is working. Emotion is a wellspring of energy, shaped in part by the social climate that drives the pace of work. Organizations with a positive vibe bring a lot of energy and enthusiasm to every task, while the beaten-down ones are dull, lifeless, and unproductive affairs.

As the new manager took over, toxicity spread across the project. Viewed through the manufacturing lens, the equipment began to shut down—some entirely, such as the original project manager who was ostracized. Other "human machines" were affected more slowly. The unseen threads of trust that connected these professionals, one to another, frayed and then snapped, impairing the social network over which information, empathy, and compassion were shared. Moreover, the antisocial behavior stimulated each producer's limbic system, the emotional brain, which cut off the cerebral cortex. The cerebral cortex is *the IT factory*, the seat of cognitive thought. In this circumstance, it was cut off by the emotional brain, which took control to focus its energy on survival tactics. Technology solutions are built one thought at a time—or not at all. With the human equipment off-line, the latter was happening.

So, here we have two efforts, accurately sized at the start, the second 30 percent less complicated than the first, yet it ended up costing twice as much to complete. This manager wasted half a million dollars of productivity in order to satisfy intrinsic emotional needs. This is a classic case of a leader blind to others: insecure, selfish, socially destructive, and highly toxic to productivity. Unfortunately, unproductive behaviors are common, especially in today's corporate environment, where many selfish, self-aggrandizing leaders rise through the ranks, often to the very top. They vary from mildly toxic to genuinely sociopathic personality types, devoid of empathy and compassion, highly destructive, yet able to cleverly manage upward, skillfully distorting the truth to stay alive and advance.

You might wonder how they can get away with it. The answer is that they have very good survival skills and wear two faces. I have seen destructive leaders tear organizations apart at every level of the corporate hierarchy and have witnessed their aftermath, as a turnaround transformation specialist who arrived to pick up the pieces. Here the toxic effects are clear. A group of dedicated, socially cohesive individuals, happy, content, working harmoniously with the business, behaving in the best interest of their partners, were suddenly torn apart and shut down by a manager trying to satisfy personal needs, not the team's. The social fabric of productivity was shredded.

Selfishness is the root cause of much lost productivity in creative solution development, where cognitive thought and positive emotions drive the work forward. This is not the case with repetitive activities, done by rote, which can occur when the worker is off-line, on autopilot. IT failure most often has social and emotional roots.

Toxic to Competitive Advantage

In this case study, the money can be quantified, yet there are many forms of loss that cannot be. In a toxic environment, filled with fear and survival tactics, absolutely no meaningful creativity is occurring. I'm talking about the type of creativity that results in a beautiful user interface, a clever solution that the business becomes enamored with, or a breakthrough approach that cuts the development time by one third; these outcomes occur only when the environment is supportive and workers are in a productive state of mind. These outcomes are meaningful to a business, often creating competitive advantage, yet you can't track the opportunity cost of what might have been. It is lost to time. What is certain is this: In an environment that isn't conducive to creativity, you get a basic, functional system. In an environment that is really toxic, you get failure.

What happened here was highly damaging—not just to the company that invested so much money but to the individuals involved. One wonders how sociopathic individuals are allowed, and sometimes even enabled, to create a wake of this size behind them. It shouldn't be allowed, and we need much greater awareness in this area, or we will continue to relive the past, where the "interchangeable parts" are dehumanized because they don't matter.

If you had been on this project, you would have seen the professionals suffering yet trying to overcome the obstacles in their path. Building a complex solution is a distinctly human drama filled with emotions and subplots. When toxic personalities and antisocial behavior are prevalent, the drama is intense.

The changing emotional state of a project's mood is a critical barometer of the outcome that will be realized; yet this human story can't be read by selfish, and therefore socially insensitive, leaders, blind to the unfolding drama, unable to feel the organization's mood, and unable to meaningfully connect with their people. If only emotional intelligence were valued; we frequently hire for IQ, then fire for lack of EQ.

Conclusion

What occurred at AnyCompany, Inc. is not unusual. IT failures, and the social pathologies that cause them, remain prevalent, and the amount of human capital investment wasted each year is staggering. Because the human factors are missing from our corporate social recipes, our professionals are left feeling unsatisfied. A collective blind spot has caused us to overlook vital ingredients, while our selfish, short-term orientation prevents us from appreciating the finesse of great cooks or the toxicity of poor ones. Even when discovered, bad cooks normally find work in another kitchen, where they continue to serve toxic meals.

To improve our return on human capital, we must acquire high-quality ingredients, thoroughly combine them, add some emotional zest, and then turn the heat up so things really cook. Not too hot, and not too cold. Today we ignore the human spice, the meals are unappetizing, and customers are unhappy.

Great kitchens do not produce great food—a cohesive and talented group of chefs and composers do. Here's a recipe you can try.

Recipe for a Productive Social System

Ingredients

Experienced composers
Servant leadership*

Human factors:
   Trust
   Social insight
   Caring
   Compassion
   Empathy
   Sharing
   Mutual respect
   Unselfishness
   Openness
   Transparency
   Humor

Directions:

Place your experienced composers in a social unit and slowly heat from below using the glow of servant leadership. As the ingredients warm up, saturate with trust so that a cohesive mixture coalesces. Now, using social insight, blend in caring, compassion, empathy, sharing, mutual respect, and unselfishness. Let stand. If the mixture darkens, quickly add openness to create transparency; if it becomes

---

*Servant leadership is critical because it is focused on the other ingredients, not itself.

too heavy, add humor to lighten it up. The warmth will cause this mix to fuse tightly together and rise. Observe closely, and remove each composer that does not gel (unmixed ingredients will create an unsatisfying meal). At this point, the social unit will really start to cook. Turn up the heat until output boils over. Share with everyone.

Yield: An incredibly satisfying meal.

Note

1. Emotional Quotient, or EQ, refers to the emotional intelligence of an individual; the words are patterned after Intelligence Quotient, IQ.

CHAPTER 6

What Are We Waiting For?

Applied Science at Work

Nothing in life is to be feared, it is only to be understood. Now is the time to understand more, so that we may fear less.

—MARIE CURIE

So much research has been done in the social sciences, psychology, and neuroscience that a strong understanding exists of the human factors that yield improved knowledge worker performance. At the moment, most of the research remains "pure science" because it has not been applied. Now is the time to embrace this human understanding and magnify our results, to unlock greatly improved returns on talent. Much remains to be learned, and, like all science, our understanding continues to evolve. But today a wealth of research provides a strong scientific basis for the practices I have successfully used to transform information technology (IT) across companies. I have no doubt that a prosocial and caring social environment is the most productive crucible for deep collaboration and great outcomes.

As one studies the academic research, the mystery of knowledge worker productivity quickly unravels. When the shared emotional needs that underpin collaboration are fully unlocked by authentic, prosocial leaders, who focus on the needs of their producers instead of their own, anything can happen. Every organization can benefit from more empathy, caring, trust, and a positive vibe. The warm glow of success can belong to every company. In this chapter, we review some of the relevant findings, although the research is vast in comparison.

Hawthorne Studies

Hawthorne effect. (noun) Psychology. A positive change in the performance of a group of persons taking part in an experiment of study due to their perception of being singled out for special consideration. Dictionary.com, June 2012.

Let's go all the way back to the 1920s. From 1924 to 1932, a team of industrial-organizational psychologists from MIT, and then Harvard, conducted a series of studies at the Hawthorne Works, a Western Electric assembly plant near Chicago. Hawthorne was an enormous complex of over 100 buildings, 40,000 workers, and 10 miles of train tracks, and was the primary assembly location for advanced telecommunications equipment for the Bell system. It made many cutting-edge products and embraced management science, as evidenced by these studies. It also produced thought leaders like W. Edwards Deming and Joseph Juran, both of whom started their careers there and dedicated their professional lives to the science of quality engineering.

The Hawthorne studies have become legendary and are frequently referenced even today. As I read the findings, they still felt fresh and alive, because the lessons have not yet been embraced and applied. Although the research is old, the findings are not dated.

The initial research team, from MIT, looked at how illumination levels affected productivity, relay assembly, supervisor training, and terminal bank wiring, to name the most noteworthy. Double-blind experiments were used, with control and noncontrol groups, so that results could be compared.

These illumination studies were conducted from 1924 to 1927 by researchers who wanted to understand the impact different lighting levels had on the productivity of women assembling relays and winding coils. In order to compare the impact of lighting changes, they divided the workers into two groups, test and control, and raised the level of lighting for the test group. Surprisingly, the productivity of both groups went up; the same occurred when the light level was lowered. Productivity increased for both groups, regardless of the lighting.

This finding confounded the team. Why would productivity go up, independent of the environmental variable? To find out, Hawthorne brought in a new team of researchers from Harvard University, led by Elton Mayo. He conducted a series of additional studies from 1928 to 1932, this time focused on the relay assembly process. In this experiment, a group of five women were moved to a separate room in order to control environment variables such as work hours and the frequency of breaks.

Relay assembly involved building mechanical relays that were used in phone switches, to connect a call across a series of central offices. (These relays were an incredible technological breakthrough that eliminated the need for switchboard operators.) Each part took about one minute to assemble, and a worker could make, on average, 2,400 per week.

The women who were in the test group, interestingly, had no supervisor. As work conditions were varied, productivity increased to 3,000 relays per person, and when work conditions were returned back to the baseline (normal), productivity remained at that elevated level. Once again, the environmental factors were not the cause of the increase.

What you find in these studies is that caring matters. The mere fact that the company cared enough about the employees to study their work environment made them feel appreciated, and they responded in kind. What goes around comes around, and in this case it was caring. That's why the level of illumination wasn't important. When management cares about your needs, your mood elevates and you feel more secure because you know someone has your back; you can relax and zone in fully on your tasks, primed with a higher level of emotional energy, drive, and engagement.

The results also reflect the increased self-esteem the women developed because they were chosen for this important effort. Mood is critical, and anything management can do to improve it yields benefits, especially if it is knowledge work that can't be directly measured. The increase is there—we know it's there—but we don't have measurement devices to tie all of this together yet. So design your culture with this feedback loop in place, and your team will perform better. It's a fact. I have witnessed it across the turnarounds and projects I have led. Caring about others matters a lot.

We also see the impact of relationships and independent control in the relay experiments. The women functioned as an independent team, which gave them control over their environment, a human need that has been shown by many studies to improve engagement, productivity, and creativity.[1] This is one of the reasons this group of workers had one third the absenteeism rate found across the rest of the factory. A feeling of control adds to an individual's sense of purpose and provides more meaning.

Mayo wrote a 600-page book on his findings, stressing the importance of the team that formed and how the strength of the relationships improved their collective performance. IT was, is, and will remain a predominantly social endeavor. When *working social*, connectedness matters, and although we've known the importance of connections for 80 years, most leaders remain uninformed about this productivity tool. Yes, emotions are a tool when it is the human infrastructure that needs performance tuning.

What I also find amazing is the research team's early understanding that human factors drive productivity, which cannot be measured but can be used. During the Hawthorne studies, it became evident that the social environment was a major influence on productivity. Yet I rarely hear anyone in Corporate talk about social chemistry, social interaction, social intelligence, social climate, and so on, and I never hear an organization referred to as a social system. Although it was already evident to academia during the industrial era, Corporate has failed to embrace, study, and implement what is well documented and well understood. Here is one quote that struck me from an essay about Elton Mayo's research:

> The existence of the informal organization . . . meant that shaping human behavior was much more complicated than the then-dominant paradigm of scientific management had led managers to believe. The social system . . . was not the product of rational engineering but of actual, deep-rooted human associations and sentiments.[2]

Although Taylorism was still in its heyday, these studies disproved one of the basic tenets of management science: that the workers would behave in their own self-interest. In fact, what mattered most was their social environment and the needs of the group. People wanted to communicate with one another and to share; they wanted to be part of a team that was open, transparent, and important. We know humans are wired for empathy and compassion because we are social animals. Over millions of years of evolution, emotions like these evolved to hold us together. (Caring, empathy, and compassion are the subject of Chapter 7.) Caring matters—use it to improve your organization or your relationships if you are an individual contributor. But if you do, sincerity is paramount, because its absence will be sensed by others, putting your trustworthiness at risk. Remain authentic and sincere in all interactions.

Pygmalion in the Classroom

> People rise and fall to meet your level of expectations for them. If you express skepticism and doubt in others, they will return your lack of confidence with mediocrity. But if you believe in them and expect them to do well, they will go the extra mile trying to do their best.
>
> —JOHN C. MAXWELL

From the Hawthorne studies, we see how paying positive attention to workers had great productive value, and this finding has since been demonstrated in other ways. In 1967, Robert Rosenthal, a Harvard researcher, and

Lenore Jacobsen, an elementary school principal, carried out a scientific study on the impact a teacher's attitude had on students' performance. Both of them felt strongly that a negative teacher bias in underprivileged neighborhoods had a deleterious effect on how the children performed. So they designed an experiment to see if it was true.

At the beginning of the school year, they gave all of the students an IQ test. Next, they randomly selected 20 percent of the student body and told the teachers these randomly selected students showed high potential. Of course, being a random sample, that wasn't true, but it set up a valid scientific experiment by providing a control group (the 80 percent) as a standard to compare the "high performers" against: By design, the teachers were unwitting participants because the experiment was kept a secret.

The question was this: By telling the teachers who the "high-performing" students were, would teachers' expectations be influenced, and would their higher expectations influence the performance of the students? Guess what, it did. At the end of the school year, a second IQ test was administered, and the randomly selected 20 percent performed better across the board. As it turns out, the teachers had become positively predisposed to the random group of high performers and expected more from them. The teacher's positive vibe energized the students to work harder and perform better. In life, people rise to meet your expectations, a phenomenon I have witnessed many times at work. They can literally feel what you think of them.

If we had a film of the teachers and students interacting, we would no doubt see how this positive predisposition influenced the teachers' behavior in both word and deed. More warmth, attention, positive comments, and encouragement naturally drove greater student achievement. So, the positive effect was the direct result of the interaction quality and the degree of caring. The outcome is very similar to the Hawthorne studies. In both cases, positive attention and caring improved individual performance. Given this finding, any manager or team member can use caring and outflowing concern at work to improve the performance of the organization or work group. Humans crave attention and want to be seen positively, which is why "saving face" is so important in many cultures. How you are perceived is vital to your standing in the social group. It feels good when management cares about you and it is motivating, as reflected in these studies. Treat your workers positively, and reap real bottom line benefits.

Empathy, Caring, and Compassion

> A human being is part of a whole, called by us the Universe. . . . He experiences himself, his thoughts and feelings, as something separated from the rest—a kind of optical delusion of his consciousness.

> This delusion is a kind of prison for us. . . . Our task must be to free ourselves from this prison by widening our circles of compassion to embrace all living creatures and the whole of nature in its beauty.
>
> —ALBERT EINSTEIN

Emotion is a survival mechanism. It evolved to enhance our individual and group odds of reproducing, thus carrying the species on. Nothing is an accident from the standpoint of evolution. Random mutations remain in the gene pool only if they confer an advantage. Emotion not only survived, it evolved into a complex mechanism to govern behavior and mood, both a compass guiding our decisions and actions, and a thermostat controlling the extent of our mood.

But emotions extend beyond the individual. As early hominids evolved, at some point they coalesced into groups with a social structure, as has been postulated by anthropologists. The evolutionary mechanism that held them together was empathy and compassion. It was a primitive time, and suffering was common because the environment was unpredictably challenging and scarcity was much more frequent. Tough times could fray the social fabric, jeopardizing everyone's survival, so these emotions existed to diminish pain and suffering and strengthen the group. Along with empathy and compassion, prosocial behaviors, such as food sharing, are also thought to have developed for the same reason: group survival. Compassion is at the heart of what it means to be human.[3] Without it, would we even exist?

For early humans, the social group was the tribe, a structure that greatly increased each member's odds of survival. A lone person would have been an easy target in a world full of stronger, faster, fiercer competitors; the tribe offered a circle of protection and an ability to hunt and gather more successfully.

From the perspective of the effectiveness of the tribe, the ability to care about others makes sense. A tribal member who was suffering was less efficient, and that diminished the resilience of the tribe. For that reason, empathy and compassion are outwardly focused emotions: unselfish, and sensitive to others' needs. These are the emotional glue that hold us together, increasing our chances of prospering. As we evolved into a social species, these emotions formed the bonds that connected individuals, one to the other.

Although the bonds that connect us today are not visible, the connections are there. Empathy and compassion lead individuals to look beyond their own needs, to see and feel the pain and suffering in others, and to act to alleviate it.

Empathy and compassion improved the survival odds of a fellow tribe member, which increased the empathetic person's own odds, because the tribe was stronger than the sum of the individual parts. But today that circuit has been cut, because we live in a world where we are literally blinded by an educational system in which emotions don't even exist. We are taught not to feel, as *understanding emotion in yourself and others* isn't part of the school curriculum, even though it is fundamental to leading a successful life, being an effective team member, and being a great leader. For any group endeavor to flourish, such as an IT project, this understanding is required, or the team never gels.

In everyday conversation, compassion and empathy are used interchangeably. From my readings, empathy is best characterized as "I feel your pain," while compassion involves a multistep process of "noticing," "feeling," and "responding."[4] So compassion is a response that tries to alleviate the pain.

These emotions are not only important group survival mechanisms, but they are vital to having an emotionally healthy organization that is highly productive. We know that when people are down, or suffering, their productivity drops. There is a direct correlation between suffering and mood; the lower the mood, the less productive energy the person creates. When you work with large groups of people, you can see the impact of lowered mood on their productivity—honestly, if you are outwardly focused on the needs of others, it is unmistakable.

Researchers have also hypothesized that compassion is a means of promoting social solidarity, which we would recognize as a healthy team at work. Caring about one another is so fundamental to the functioning of IT, or any group endeavor, that we must encourage our workers, and team members, to behave unselfishly, helping others when they need it. Moreover, people have a need to be noticed, and compassion clearly makes workers feel they have been seen and recognized by management and their peers. This makes them feel much less isolated, which is an important part of helping them feel comfortable, so that they can relax, think, and produce.

Empathy by itself is very important even if it is less of a response than compassion. I have always tuned into my workers' moods and would immediately stop someone and say, "You look a little down. Is there anything I can do to help?" The answer was normally "No, but thank you very much for noticing," at which point we would chat briefly, and the person would walk away with a smile. The worker's mood had been lifted; the act of noticing had alleviated pain and made him or her feel valued. Doing this is not only easy (of course, it must be sincere) but important to the success of the organization. More important, as an executive or leader, you are modeling a prosocial behavior that others will emulate. It is okay to care about others—that is an important message to send, as it diminishes your workers' reluctance to show and talk about emotion.

So empathy and compassion and, at a higher level, caring about others are fundamental to organizational performance. They should be encouraged and are very powerful aids to collaboration and productivity. According to the research,[5] these attitudes are linked to a wide range of positive behaviors, attitudes, and feelings in companies, and should be recognized for what they are: important lubricants that remove social friction and pain from the organization.

How could this not be a good thing? We can't measure the after-effects of an act of kindness, but a lack of measurement doesn't lessen its importance.

Last, the research identifies three ways of compassionate response in the workplace: providing time and flexibility, material support, and emotional support.[6] I have seen all of them unlock the productivity of the workforce.

I cannot say enough about work–life balance. I have rolled out flexible work arrangements in three different companies and each time achieved much higher levels of productivity. Why? Because workers become mentally preoccupied and stressed out when they can't attend to something important in their personal lives, such as elder care, child care, visiting a teacher, going to the doctor, and so on. This mental preoccupation diverts precious cognitive resources away from problem solving to worrying. If you provide a flexible work structure, then all workers can schedule and attend to these important responsibilities, freeing their minds and emotions to fully engage while at work. Everything needs a compartment of its own.

Another important aspect regarding empathy comes from neuroscience. Everyone has a dopamine center in their brain. Many people are familiar with this because exercise results in a feeling of well-being when dopamine, a neurotransmitter, is released into the bloodstream. This dopamine response is frequently referred to in the literature. What is less well known is that empathy also causes activity in the dopamine center of the brain. So empathy has its own built-in reward, a response that must have evolved to increase the frequency of this behavior, thus increasing survival rates.

Organizational Citizenship Behavior

> In helping others, we shall help ourselves, for whatever good we give out completes the circle and comes back to us.
>
> —FLORA EDWARDS

After successfully transforming IT across corporations, I realized that the antidote to socially toxic organizations was prosocial leadership coupled with shared prosocial behaviors. This topic is so important that Chapter 9 is devoted to it.

To transform organizational behavior, I established ground rules in my town halls and leadership meetings by communicating that the basis of our success would be building a trust-based community where meaningful collaboration and prosocial behaviors would infuse every interaction. These behaviors included sharing/helping, caring for one another (empathy and compassion), openness/acceptance of others' personalities and ideas, complete transparency (no hidden agendas), and an absence of blame. Ultimately, the goal was to create harmony, because that is a powerful driver of collaborative productivity.

Most workers understood and embraced these notions. Ultimately I found it necessary to define a behavioral model that specified what behaviors yielded the best interaction-based outcomes.

Orchestrating the right behaviors was a powerful culture builder. When I dug into the academic research, I found an entire area of academic study devoted to this. Organizational citizenship behavior (OCB) was first proposed by Bateman and Organ in 1983 to recognize organizationally beneficial behaviors that are not explicitly tied to a role and which employees can voluntarily withhold without regard to sanctions or formal incentives.[7] This was further defined by Dennis Organ in his 1988 book, *The Good Soldier Syndrome*, as "individual behavior that is discretionary, not directly or explicitly recognized by the formal reward system, and that in the aggregate promotes the effective functioning of the organization."[8] Organ's findings are spot on, especially in any highly collaborative endeavor.

In my studies, I found an overlapping area in the research: prosocial organizational behavior. Suffice it to say, there is broad agreement that behaviors that help increase others' success are powerful, as has been my experience. Personally, I prefer the term *prosocial organizational behavior*, because it specifies precisely what type of behavior is productive in an inherently social undertaking like a cross-functional IT project.

There are many prosocial actions an individual can take that help fellow team members, improve the mood of the organization, or support the department as a whole. When everyone embraces the notion that success in IT is collective, then prosocial behaviors predominate, and productivity improves dramatically. Interactions become more fluid, a positive vibe grows, and individual burdens are easily carried when shared across many workers. The following quote captures the flavor of what prosocial OCB is all about:

> The list included such gestures as constructive statements about the department, expression of personal interest in the work of others, suggestions for improvement, training new people, respect for the spirit as well as the letter of housekeeping rules, care for organizational property, and attendance . . . well beyond enforceable levels.[9]

Behaving prosocially goes beyond helping others, pointing out positives, and going the extra mile without being asked; it also means shunning negative and unproductive behaviors. Anyone who has managed or participated in projects, teams, and organizations intimately understands how detrimental it is to be inconsiderate of your coworkers. I have witnessed selfish and toxic behaviors many times so they remain prevalent even today. Although OCB researchers posit that workers should voluntarily *refrain* from negative behaviors like finding fault and showing resentment, these antisocial behaviors should not be allowed, period. They destroy group productivity by undermining collaboration and yield a much lower return on human capital. From that perspective, they are destructive. We have clear policies against discrimination and sexual harassment, and we seek "customer intimacy," yet we allow ostracism, blame, and many toxic and destructive behaviors in the workplace. It is time to proscribe these as well, by defining and promoting which OCB's are productive and which are unproductive. That way, coworkers have the right to stop damaging behavior by pointing it out and saying "That's not allowed here." Remember, we aren't talking about a love-in, but workplace productivity. If you could improve a process by removing a wasteful step, you would not hesitate. Treat behavior the same way: Eliminate the unproductive behaviors and encourage the productive ones.

Mood Is Contagious

> Never make your most important decisions when you are in your worst moods. Wait. Be patient. The storm will pass. Spring will come.
>
> —Robert H. Shuller

I have told many people that research proves mood is contagious. They all say, "I've always felt that was true." This is something we have all experienced, and we now know it isn't an opinion but a fact. Mood is a key driver of the energy level, confidence, and resilience of an organization. It is critical to success and productivity. The higher up the leader, the more positive or detrimental their mood is.

A few things are very important. First, research suggests that "leaders are more likely to be transmitters of moods and subordinates are more likely to be receivers of moods."[10] This makes sense since humans are very sensitive to social hierarchy and will model their mood and behavior after their leaders. One time an executive from Microsoft was being interviewed, and he related how Bill Gates would rock back and forth at meetings. By the end of a meeting, the whole room would be doing the same. Must have been funny to see, but it is a powerful insight into how we model our leader's behaviors. Subordinates are in fact the receivers.

The quote below comes from a research study titled *The Contagious Leader*, which is worth reading, especially if you are a leader. But the summary makes all the points:

> The present study examined the effects of leaders' mood on (a) the mood of individual group members, (b) the affective tone of groups,

and (c) group processes: coordination, effort expenditure, and task strategy. On the basis of a mood contagion model, the authors found that when leaders were in a positive mood, in comparison to a negative mood, (a) individual group members experienced more positive and less negative mood, and (b) groups had a more positive and less negative affective tone. The authors also found that groups with leaders in a positive mood exhibited more coordination and expended less effort than did groups with leaders in a negative mood.[11]

Mood is so critical that maintaining an upbeat attitude, especially in the darkest of times, is an incredible driver of productivity. The energy level of every person rises as "receivers" pick up the high-energy signal and in turn spread it to their teams. It works. I've seen its positive impact on groups and organizations throughout my career. Keep your mood and spirit up, and you and your teams will prosper.

This is science; the impact of mood on productivity has been studied and measured. Nancy Rothbard, a David Pottruck associate professor of management at Wharton, found that call center employees who arrived at work in a negative mood were 10 percent less productive all day.[12] For IT, this is even worse, because progress requires creativity. A negative mood impacts the creative process, and it is difficult to measure because much of the work isn't repetitive. Managers can positively impact the mood of these individuals by transmitting caring, positive, upbeat energy, as shown in this study. Additionally, showing empathy and caring will help even more. If you lift workers' spirits, the dividend is improved productivity throughout the entire day.

Limbic System

> Our civilization is still in a middle stage, scarcely beast, in that it is no longer guided by instinct, scarcely human in that it is not yet wholly guided by reason.
>
> —THEODORE DREISER

The limbic system contains the central wiring for emotion and is our midbrain. A small gland inside the midbrain called the amygdala is best described as a threat sensor. It has been studied for many, many years, and I remember as a biology major reading how the sympathetic nervous system regulated flight-or-fight reactions. Our knowledge today is much greater because magnetic resonance imaging has allowed scientists to conduct experiments while peering into the brain to see which areas light up under differing circumstances. As it turns out, humans are wired for survival, and over 90 percent of the wiring in the midbrain exists for that purpose. From an evolutionary standpoint, this makes great sense: If you don't survive, your genes are eliminated from the gene pool. Survival had to be priority #1.

As humans evolved, the world was a physically dangerous place, but modern civilization has changed the nature of the threat. Now the key to survival is maintaining an income so you can secure your food and shelter. Many things at work stimulate the limbic system, and these have a very damaging effect on productivity. Let's quickly examine why.

When a threat is perceived, the limbic system releases adrenaline into the bloodstream, which tenses muscles, raises the heartbeat, increases blood flow, cuts off higher-order thinking, and focuses the mind fully on the threat at hand. In any type of knowledge work, thinking effectively stops. It's the same as slowing down or even fully shutting down a network; as most cell phone owners have experienced, the network is there but not responding.

> We now understand that higher-level thinking is more likely to occur in the brain of a student who is emotionally secure than in the brain of a student who is scared, upset, anxious, or stressed.
>
> —Thomas S. Mawhinney and Laura L. Sagan

The threat can be as simple as a hostile manager attacking you verbally or publicly berating you. These attacks on your pride and security have negative and long-lasting consequences. If the attack is serious enough, the limbic system can remain aroused for a long period of time, leaving the individual unable to think clearly or focus on work. Just because people are sitting at their desks is in itself meaningless. The question is whether they are in a productive state of mind, as the mind is the tool that must be functioning in order for work to be done. I always laugh at the almost irrelevant notion of attendance. Many people are present but not productive in modern companies; the same can be said about so many meetings. So, what should we focus on? Taking attendance, or attending to our people?

What types of antisocial behavior stimulate an *amygdala hijacking* (of the mind and body), as it is called in science? There are many, but here is a partial list:

- Blame
- Hidden agendas
- Deceit
- Combative behavior
- Intimidation
- Fear

- Threats
- Public embarrassment
- Humiliation
- Criticism
- Emotional aggression
- Conflict
- Punishment
- Untrustworthy behavior
- Insincerity
- Betrayal
- Ostracism

I have witnessed all of these in socially toxic workplaces. The amygdala provides a range of responses based on the severity of the threat. All of these responses lie on a spectrum from minimal to severe. Being subjected to recurring antisocial behavior causes the neurotransmitters to remain in the blood, leaving people on constant alert. Ultimately this causes an individual to become stressed out, impacting two primary IT tools, cognition and memory, and thus greatly reducing productivity.

Stress has been extensively studied, so we know with certainty that an emotionally toxic environment affects workers' mental and emotional health. Dating all the way back to scientific findings in the 1950s, the cognitive impacts of stress include a loss of focus, flight of ideas, impaired judgment, an inability to concentrate, impaired memory, and constant worrying or rumination, leaving the individual distracted and unable to think about his or her work. It has also been shown through more recent studies that healthy individuals who had endured routine stress had less gray matter in their prefrontal cortex, an area known to regulate our emotions. This shrinkage indicates a loss of neurons that diminishes the individual's ability to cope with future stress because they are depleted.

From an emotional perspective, a stressful work environment can leave an individual feeling overwhelmed and out of control; it can lead to low energy levels, producing fatigue, reduced drive, and less ambition; it can increase irritability, leading to a short fuse and outbursts of anger; it can produce loss of confidence and lower self-esteem, impairing one's ability to start challenging tasks; it can lower the desire for social interaction, causing the person to withdraw from coworkers; it can make one moody, negative, and unpredictable, such that coworkers stay away. When you consider the range of emotional and cognitive harm, the productivity impact is self-evident. Leaders need to minimize job-related stress so that the human infrastructure remains optimized for work.

These manifestations are based on the intensity of the threat and can be partially or fully expressed. Nevertheless, little high-value IT work will take place when the limbic system remains stimulated and stress begins to show. With the human infrastructure shutting down, collaboration wanes; because of the low trust levels that characterize these work environments, productivity plummets and remains low. It is an incredible loss of investment, but since productivity isn't measured, leaders who create these toxic environments are typically good at kissing up. By wearing two faces, they can last for years, until the failures can no longer be explained away or blamed on others. It takes two to three years to reach that point.

We also know from research that the amygdala is always scanning its environment to spot a threat. The image of any individual who threatens you more than once is imprinted in your mind, and their mere presence is all that is needed to stimulate your threat sensor. Pavlov's research into conditioned responses is famous, and often quoted. Fear conditioning in humans works the same way, and can be long lasting. Repeated threats and provocations from a belligerent and blame-oriented manager will quickly be imprinted on the brain of the subordinate, so that the manager's physical presence is all that is needed to stress the individual. "Not only is fear conditioning quick, it is also very long lasting. In fact, there is little forgetting when it comes to conditioned fear. The passing of time is not enough to get rid of it."[13]

Once again, the scientific underpinning of what many have experienced is right here. How often has the mere presence of toxic, antisocial peers or leaders caused the mood of a room to change as they enter, or the hair to stand up on your neck as they pass you in the hallway? They have been imprinted as a threat, and this fear-conditioned response isn't going to go away until they are gone. What I have noticed, therefore, is that the first step in the healing process is the removal of these socially damaging personality types.

Maslow: Humanism in the Workplace

Classic economic theory, based as it is on an inadequate theory of human motivation, could be revolutionized by accepting the reality of higher human needs, including the impulse to self actualization and the love for the highest values.

—ABRAHAM MASLOW

Abraham Maslow, best known for his hierarchy of human needs, is also the father of humanistic psychology. Although a behaviorist by training, he quickly realized that outside of a laboratory setting, where controlled experiments yielded predictable results, behaviorism couldn't be applied. He wrote in his journal:

> Behaviorism has done a lot. . . . But its fatal flaw is that it's good for the lab. . . . It's useless at home with your kids and wife and friends. It does not generate an adequate . . . conception of human nature. It's not an adequate guide to living, to values, to choice.[14]

Maslow was committed to bringing the whole person, the complete human being, with thoughts and emotions, into the mainstream of psychology. He took a positive view of humankind and its potential for greatness if properly cultivated and expressed. Maslow was ahead of his time because he didn't believe that your life was predetermined, as the behaviorists preached. He felt humans had choices and that, given an opportunity to learn, grow, and develop, their potential was unlimited; he also believed in the basic goodness of humanity, and he has been proven right, as behaviorism has fallen from the mainstream.

Maslow proposed that people need to meet their basic physiological needs first (food, clothing, shelter), followed by safety and then love and belongingness, which opens the way to self-esteem and ultimately self-actualization or, as I like to view it, fulfilling your potential. He was a firm believer that people should focus on the positive aspects of others, instead of the negative, and rejected the foundational beliefs of Freudian psychoanalysis and behaviorism, which taught that people are nothing but bags of symptoms to be studied. His beliefs are more closely aligned with today's positive psychology than the schools of thought that preceded him. His hierarchy is shown in Figure 6.1.

My experience has shown me that Maslow's humanistic hierarchy of needs contains a recipe for unlocking the talent of your workforce. I have seen it in action when I enter toxic environments where fear is prevalent. When driving a turnaround transformation, you need to work your way up the top four rows of the pyramid, beginning with safety. Each layer you move through produces higher levels of productivity and defines a clean strategy. It is tragic that the teachings of these great minds have been ignored in the world of work, but if you want to break from the pack and maximize the productivity of your knowledge workers, you can.

Figure 6.2 shows what my hierarchy of productivity needs looks like, along with the human factors prevalent at each layer.

In order for productivity to happen, an emotionally safe environment is absolutely required. As noted earlier, there are many organizations with great attendance, where people are physically present yet mentally absent. It's frankly the norm, but since attendance is fine, management can point to it as an indication of engagement; good work, you get another "A" for attendance.

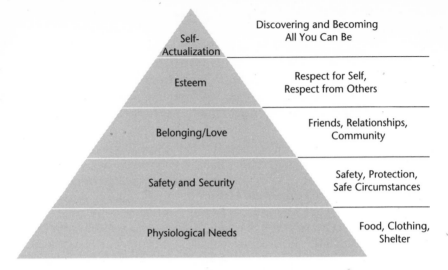

Figure 6.1 Maslow's Hierarchy of Needs

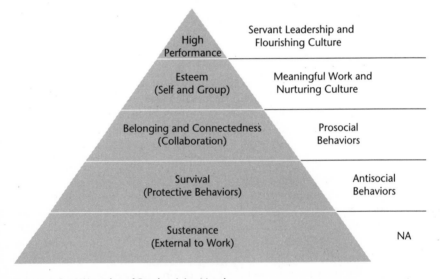

Figure 6.2 Hierarchy of Productivity Needs

Work cultures stuck at level 2 exhibit antisocial behaviors, where the mixture of leadership personalities and cultural norms directly determine their frequency. The more toxic the blend, the more these behaviors threaten the staff's welfare, financial security, and survival. In response, protective behaviors become prevalent as workers fight to hang on, resulting in survival-level output, an organization's lowest possible return on human capital. Engagement stays at low levels, and extrinsic motivators, such as fear of reprisal and of public admonishment and the simple need to endure, drive projects forward. Distrust is prevalent, and without trust, true collaboration occurs in isolated pockets, among people who have bonded with one another to counter the emotional stress and find safety. These social systems are highly unproductive affairs, where emotionless zombies can be seen going through the motions, wasting their creative potential on mere survival tactics. I have walked into cultures like this many times, and Frederick Taylor's notion of "workers soldiering on" often came to mind. Yes, just one more step, totally disengaged, haphazardly moving forward. It's motion without momentum.

As toxic forces are removed, the work environment begins to heal. By stressing the need for trust, openness, mutual respect, and collaboration, the organization moves through level 2 and breaks into level 3. The antisocial forces that caused the human infrastructure to shut down are replaced by a culture that is neutral, almost in a wait-and-see state. Productivity begins to flow, and as trust replaces distrust, cautious bonds form, linking groups of co-creators together. Collaboration and sharing, openness, candor, and teamwork open the lines of communication, and the social network begins to come alive. At this point, the emotional climate is improving, and if the right actions continue, progress continues through to level 4.

In level 4, deep bonds begin to form. Trust grows, and prosocial behaviors, such as helping one another, sharing information, encouragement, thankfulness, empathy, and compassion, begin to operate more widely. The "smile index" grows stronger, as workers find esteem in their work, in their contributions, in the warmth of their connections, and in team outcomes; mutual respect for one another blossoms. It's not a love-in, as work brings with it stressful deadlines. But this time what intrinsically motivates the professionals is personal fear of failure and loss of self-esteem rather than fear of reprisal. They can relax, enjoy what they are doing, be creative, and share in the glow of a positive social climate.

To break through to level 5, people and teams must be supertight, in roles that are well matched to their aptitude and personality type. It takes a long time for people to find their way to this level. Sometimes they need to switch careers or move to a different part of the organization. But through a process of continuous organizational improvement and filtering, institutional knowledge grows, social capital accumulates, and strong relationships turn into highly productive interactions so that innovation starts to bubble. This is a truly high-performing culture. The term *organizational effectiveness* is bandied about, and human resource areas preach it, but most organizations don't understand the impact of behavior and emotion on the productivity of their knowledge workers, whose primary tools are mind and emotion, woven together to form a social network of productivity.

Unquestionably, human understanding has high productive value. The job of management is to acquire the best talent and create an environment where it *literally flourishes*. How to do this is the key. Maslow was way ahead of his time, and he lectured on the need for humanistic practices (positive motivation achieved through peak experiences that gave way to self-actualization) in the workplace because he saw how higher levels of his pyramid would benefit corporations. During good times, management sees no need to rock the boat—just pass go and collect $200; but today, with dissatisfaction rife, engagement pinned at frighteningly low levels, and the social fabric of society and corporations fraying, new solutions must be sought. I think our social roots and craftsmen past is indeed prologue. We already know all we need to know. It's just a matter of applying it. Prosocial, unselfish, caring cultures will predominate, because they unlock the full human potential needed to create competitive advantage for corporations.

Working Memory

> The productivity of work is not the responsibility of the worker, but of the manager.
>
> —PETER DRUCKER

In IT, we are always worried if machines have adequate memory, but the question doesn't come up if the "machine" is an employee or consultant. That's their problem, right?

The fact is, it has been known for a long time that humans have limited memory to handle conscious tasks. As limited as this memory is, it can be constrained further by environmental/cultural issues. If you take the time to study this topic, you find that the prefrontal cortex holds short-term memory for tasks you are consciously working on. In contrast, most of what we do is controlled by the subconscious, which has programs for all of the repetitive, complex activities, such as driving a car, playing sports, walking up and down the stairs, social signaling (smiles, nods, eyes raised), and so on; in contrast to the conscious mind, its capacity is vast.

Our conscious capacity has been known for a very long time, dating back at least to early research by Bell Labs when researchers studied how to structure the national dial plan. The goal: Define a dial plan with the longest number of digits people could hold in short-term memory. They found that human working memory is 7, plus or minus 2. So they arrived at 10 digits as the largest workable format, composed of a three-digit area code, a three-digit prefix, and a line number. From the standpoint of how our memory works, an area code is actually handled as one item because the mind remembers chunks, and the prefix (next three digits) was also a chunk. With the line number, you have 10 digits but six things to remember, something most people can easily do. The research was brilliant for its day because the dial plan has lasted for over 100 years, advances in switching notwithstanding.

When you are managing "human equipment," the operator's manual is clear: Don't assign people too many concurrent tasks. IT is a thinking business—knowing how to get the most out of your people matters. Also here is another instance where a negative, unsafe culture shuts down the machines. "Circuits from the limbic brain to the prefrontal lobes mean that the signals of strong emotion—anxiety, anger, and the like—can create neural static, sabotaging the ability of the prefrontal lobe to maintain working memory."[15] If working memory is impaired, an IT professional is not going to make progress on cognitive tasks. That's a fact I have witnessed many times when being called in to cope with the toxic aftermath of an organizational sociopath.

The fact that today's management doesn't understand the basics of the human infrastructure, such that a toxic manager can shut down the entire "cognitive factory," is a waste of human capital. Since the emotional damage is not visible, these people are allowed to continue until their antisocial behavior causes visible consequences—typically a collective failure of the organization to deliver on their commitments.

Way before these toxic leaders are fired, everyone in the organization and everyone connected to it is talking about what a cancer they are. But, being bullies, they usually get away with it because they are highly confrontational and will seek to destroy anyone who tells the truth—especially those who are under their direct control. If these toxic individuals walked into the data center and powered it down, they would be fired on the spot because it would be seen as a malicious, damaging act that was very costly to the company. Guess what? They do it all the time—the equipment just happens to be human!

Mirror Neurons

The great gift of human beings is that we have the power of empathy, we can all sense a mysterious connection to each other.

—MERYL STREEP

Much has been written about mirror neurons since a research paper described their role and action in 1996, as described on the following page.

Although how many roles they play in life is still debated in scientific circles, much is known, and they are at the core of our social consciousness. If you do any reading at all, you will see they were discovered by an Italian scientist, Giacomo Rizzolatti, who was using macaque monkeys for neuroscientific research.

Sandra Blakeslee wrote a great article on this topic for the *New York Times* in 2006. In addition, there is a wealth of research and articles available on the Web. To quote Blakeslee: "[I]f the findings, published in 1996, surprised most scientists, recent research has left them flabbergasted. Humans, it turns out, have mirror neurons that are far smarter, more flexible and more highly evolved than any of those found in monkeys, a fact that scientists say reflects the evolution of humans' sophisticated social abilities."[16] Thus, at our core, we are social beings, and the more we learn, the more we understand how vital being social is to our humanity.

What mirror neurons actually do is allow us to feel what other people are feeling. It is the source of empathy and compassion, because another person's feeling is literally re-created inside of us. Like everything else in life, some people have a lot of mirror neurons, and some have a little. It is always a spectrum. "We are exquisitely social creatures," Dr. Rizzolatti said. "Our survival depends on understanding the actions, intentions and emotions of others." He continued: "Mirror neurons allow us to grasp the minds of others not through conceptual reasoning but through direct simulation. By feeling, not by thinking."[17]

First off, humans expect, based on our social wiring, that other members of the "tribe" will show empathy and compassion. When they don't, people immediately distrust them and feel uncomfortable around them, as their intentions could be damaging. Every organization needs to encourage people to feel and use their feelings to improve team connectedness so that collaboration can increase.

However, what's most interesting to me is understanding these mirror neurons as a source of rapport. People having a conversation will unconsciously begin to mirror what the other individual is doing. This was documented and written about way before Rizzolatti's research was published in 1996. If you lack this skill, then you create an undercurrent of tension because you are out of sync with the other person; if you have a strong sense of feeling about others, you will literally feel the tension, because something is not right. There are other reasons for this, as when words and body language do not match. Either way, if someone is in a collaborative role where rapport really matters, or in a leadership position where trust is a critical currency, being emotionally in tune with your social environment is critical. If that individual lacks these skills, then they have a critical deficit. My take is that these professionals perform best in individual contributor roles.

Other Thoughts

There is so much pertinent research that I don't have room to include it in this book. We could:

- Delve into the scientific proof that *laughter* is productive and a great aid to creativity (people don't just like to laugh, they need to!).
- Examine how *cognitive dissonance* has been known since 1957, showing how people cling to a belief even when confronted with incontrovertible proof to the contrary (as a leader, accept this, and don't hold this behavior against people when you see it).
- Go through the well-documented studies showing how an interruption can cost 15 minutes of lost "cognitive flow" (is your work environment productive?).
- Examine Gallup findings that people with a friend at work are 30 percent more engaged (shouldn't you encourage the building of strong relationships?).
- Consider other Gallup findings that if your boss is your friend, you are 30 percent more productive (leaders really do need to sincerely bond with their people).
- See how leaders who are vulnerable and humble are much more successful.
- Learn how *toxic handlers* (covered in Chapter 7) are invaluable to maintaining an upbeat team mood and spirit, especially in the face of disappointment or toxicity.

The list of research is enormous. Read a lot; learn about your "equipment", and apply it at work. Whether you are an individual contributor and team member or a leader, you will prosper.

Notes

1. There have been many research studies into autonomy and control and its impact on work. In a study of employee engagement in Canada by Psychometrics (www.psychometrics.com/docs/engagement_study.pdf), control was one of the highest-rated influencers on engagement and salary one of the lowest. This is consistent across many studies, and you can find tons freely available by searching the Web.
2. Michel Anteby and Rakesh Khurana, "A New Vision," Harvard Business School. Available at www.library.hbs.edu/hc/hawthorne/anewvision.html.
3. G. Himmelfarb, "The Idea of Compassion: The British vs. the French Enlightenment," *Public Interest* 145 (2001): 3–24.

4. Jason M. Kanov, Sally Maitlis, Monica C. Worline, Jane E. Dutton, Peter J. Frost, and Jacoba M. Lilius, "Compassion in Organizational Life," *American Behavioral Scientist* 47 (2004): 808–827. See pp. 9–13. I highly recommend this journal article, which is available at webuser.bus.umich.edu/janedut/Compassion/Comp%20Organ%20Life.pdf.

5. Ibid. See p. 4.

6. Jacoba M. Lilius et al., "Compassion Revealed: What We Know About Compassion at Work." See p. 7. Available at http://webuser.bus.umich.edu/janedut/Compassion/POS_Compassion_Chapter_FINAL%20(1).pdf.

7. Dennis W. Organ, "The Motivational Basis of Organizational Citizenship Behavior," *Research in Organizational Behavior* 12 (1990): 46.

8. J. P. Sharma, N. Bajpai, and U. Holani, "Organizational Citizenship Behavior in Public and Private Sector and Its Impact on Job Satisfaction: A Comparative Study in Indian Perspective," *International Journal of Business and Management* 6 (January 2011): 67. Recommended as a quick read with a good overview of OCB for those new to the subject. Available at ccsenet.org/journal/index.php/ijbm/article/download/7068/6515.

9. Organ, "The Motivational Basis of Organizational Citizenship Behavior."

10. T. Sy, S. Cote, and R. Saavedra, "The Contagious Leader," *Journal of Applied Psychology* 90, no. 2 (2005): 295–305, p. 296.

11. Ibid., 295.

12. N. Rothbard, "Mood and Productivity: Undoing a Bad Start," *Wharton Work* (April 2011), 1.

13. J. LeDoux, *The Emotional Brain* (New York: Touchstone, 1996), 146.

14. N. Seel, *Encyclopedia of Sciences and Learning* (New York: Springer, 2012), 1472.

15. Daniel Goleman, *Emotional Intelligence* (New York: Bantam, 1995), 27.

16. Sandra Blakeslee, "Cells That Read Minds," *New York Times* On-Line, January 10, 2006. Available at www.nytimes.com/2006/01/10/science/10mirr.html?pagewanted=all.

17. Ibid.

CHAPTER 7

Empathy and Compassion

The Socially Cohesive and Resilient Organization

Could a greater miracle take place than for us to look through each other's eyes for an instant?

—HENRY DAVID THOREAU

Empathy and compassion are frequently written about in academic research. As a leader, I normally put these under the broader heading of "caring," an umbrella term that encompasses caring deeply about one another (empathy and compassion), caring about the mission, and caring about the quality of the collective outcome. I have found that using the word *caring* plays better in Corporate, as its leaders aren't yet ready to openly talk about emotions, especially empathy and compassion. Yet in information technology (IT), caring matters, especially caring about one another, because IT is mentally and emotionally demanding. Since the value of an emotionally supportive work environment is poorly understood, frequently it is managed in socially insensitive ways. This in turn cascades into higher levels of stress, sacrifice, and suffering among IT professionals.

Empathy and compassion strengthen the degree of connectedness helping unite an organization. To IT, these are critical. As I've noted many times, great IT outcomes are directly related to the degree of social cohesion that individuals, teams, and cross-functional units achieve. Based on my personal experience, empathy and compassion are critical emotional skills that fall high on the list of highly desirable prosocial behaviors, but their productive impact is neither seen nor measured. These emotions are subtle, working their magic so quietly that they are neither valued nor understood.

One of the negative outgrowths of Taylor's scientific management was how it unintentionally removed the humanity remaining in work. This unintended consequence of a focus on process versus people is still with us to this day. Clearly, humans are wired to care for one another as a species—it's our shared evolutionary heritage. As human understanding of this fact ebbed away, the emphasis moved from social to capital, creating a focus on economic outcomes. This rejection and betrayal of humanity led to unionization, a mirror image of the selfishness engendered by capitalism, just pathologically focused on the needs of the workers at the expense of the business. Two wrongs don't make a right, but when workers are threatened, they will engage in protective behaviors at both individual and group levels. Unions are just group protective behavior.

In Chapter 6, you read about some of the science behind the emotional and neurological forces that unite us. It is clear that these emotions, and mirror neurons, evolved to unite us and hold us together. Caring about others is not only nice, it is absolutely necessary to create a tight social weave. The evolutionary underpinnings of both empathy and compassion are clear: Some glue was needed to bring people together, and an ability to notice suffering and pain in others formed a bond, or attachment, between individuals. Shared pain and thoughtfulness are powerful. I have seen them work many times to release people's burdens so that they could begin to work productively, focusing on the task at hand rather than what was weighing them down. Whether recognized or functioning in the shadows, the caring emotions are an important part of building a healthy social climate. Let's look more deeply into this.

The Toxic Handler: Empathy and Compassion in Action

Empathy is like giving someone a Psychological Hug.

—Lawrence J. Bookbinder

Empathy and compassion can be clearly seen in the role of the *toxic handler*. For years as a leader, I would always tell people that one of my jobs was to "be the umbrella, stopping the rain from above from falling on them." This made so much sense to me. There was tremendous productive value in ensuring my teams weren't mentally distracted. Often I rephrased messages that came down insensitively from above or were poorly framed in a town hall meeting by a socially unintelligent leader. Most of the time, because I was trusted, people calmed down and went back to work. That said, I never incorrectly translated a message, because people have a right to complete transparency. You can't hide reality, nor do you want to lose credibility by lying about what is happening. When the truth was indeed negative, I would chat about what it meant with whoever wanted to speak about it privately. Some would accept it, and some would seek peace. Whatever the motive or need, I was happy to satisfy it so that we could all go back to work.

In my research, I found that the toxic handler is a well-documented form of empathy and compassion, and an incredibly important organizational role, more necessary than ever given the high pressures of today. A great *Harvard Business Review* article titled "The Toxic Handler: Organizational Hero—and Casualty" reveals the scientific basis for the importance of this role and how it should be rewarded and encouraged.[1] Today these individuals are for the most part unseen and not valued because of our blindness to the human factors that exist in organizations.

For this article, the authors interviewed and observed 70 executives who were either toxic handlers themselves or who had one working for them. The authors defined a *toxic handler* as "a manager who voluntarily shoulders the sadness, frustration, bitterness, and anger that are endemic to organizational life."[2] This role is important, and every manager and coworker should strive to reduce workplace stress so that work can flow smoothly. Any stress that isn't dealt with causes work to slow further, in turn building more pressure, a vicious cycle if not short-circuited. The work of the toxic handler is absolutely vital to success when large teams have to collaborate and overcome every obstacle, even those erected unintentionally by the organization. Toxicity is frequent, and deadly to productivity.

In the article, the authors provide further insight into how beneficial these unsung heroes are. "[Great] ideas dry up when people are hurting or when they are focused on organizational dysfunction. It is toxic handlers who frequently step in and absorb others' pain so that high-quality work continues to get done."[3] Chapter 12 deals specifically with how to build an environment that is conducive to creativity and innovation. Don't ignore the value of workers like this.

Research identifies five specific ways in which the impact of toxic handlers is felt:

1. **They listen empathetically**. In essence, they always have time for people who need to talk. In fact, I always told people my door was open, and I meant it. As a result, team members stopped by to chat. Sometimes they needed reassurance, and others just wanted face time. Either way, I was a very good listener. Most important, I would never judge why they came, what was bothering them, or how important it was. All that mattered was it was important enough for them to stop by. Research confirms that being nonjudgmental is critical.

2. **They suggest solutions**. Compassion is all about helping. Alleviate the pain if you can by listening, but help directly by intervening if

that is what it takes. Every minute a professional is cognitively off the air, you are losing partial or full productivity. As a leader, you must address this for the welfare of the team.

3. **They work behind the scenes to prevent pain**. If you know someone is going to face a situation that is very unpleasant, intervene if doing so makes sense. Preventing a painful situation is better than dealing with the aftermath, so be alert, and be proactive.

4. **They carry the confidence of others**. To be in this role, you must be absolutely trustworthy. If not, who will ever come to you? And, rest assured, if you violate an individual's trust, it will spread. Humans have tremendous survival skills, and one such skill is group members alerting others to danger. Sometimes this is referred to as gossip, but it is how we are wired, and bad news travels fast. Be a confidant.

5. **They reframe difficult messages**. As just noted, reframing difficult messages is valuable—especially if you work in an organization where a senior leader or the chief executive doesn't understand the feelings of others. It can keep you busy, but the dividends are high.

One other thing to understand is that you need to have empathy for the toxic handlers as well. Their role and compassion don't come without a price. "Managing organizational pain is vital to the health of the enterprise—but at great cost to the health of the toxic handlers themselves."[4]

To me, these people are very, very important to an IT organization, or any organization for that matter. Observe and listen, and you will find out who they are. Thank them for voluntarily taking on this role. Note how important it is. It will lessen their burden. And, remember, behavior is contagious. People will copy what you do if you are the leader, so spreading this toxic handling behavior through the organization is very beneficial.

Dysfunctional Organizations Have Less Time for Compassion

Beware the barrenness of a busy life.

—SOCRATES

Organizations that are suffering from dysfunction are caught in a downward spiral. As dysfunction increases, work slows, and as work slows, pressure increases. Deadlines fall behind, tasks build up, and people need more emotional support than ever. But research shows very clearly that people in a rush are least likely to help.

In a study on this topic, John M. Darley and C. Daniel Batson designed an experiment at Princeton Theological Seminary that used 67 seminary students as subjects who were told they were needed to do a reading.[5] When the subjects arrived at the location they were instructed to come to, they were asked to practice some scripted text and then told to proceed to another building where they would be recorded. Interestingly, half the students were told they would be doing a reading on the parable of the Good Samaritan and the other half something else. Along the way, they passed a man slumped in a doorway, in obvious need of help. The purpose of the study: Find out how many would stop.

To understand the impact of pressure, a time variable was added, and the students were broken into three groups: High Hurry (you're late, go right now); Intermediate Hurry (they are ready for you but no need to rush); and, last, Low Hurry (they aren't ready; you can take your time).

The research showed that 63 percent of the Low Hurry group stopped, followed by 45 percent of the Intermediate Hurry, and only 10 percent of the High Hurry subjects. Whether they were giving a talk on the Good Samaritan or not had no impact on their helping behavior. The time pressure led them to behave selfishly.

The lesson for work is clear: There are always pressures, so modeling the right behavior for your teams or coworkers will greatly increase the bias to help. More important, designing a culture that is productive, collaborative, supportive, and creative greatly improves the flow of work, reducing the incidence of high-hurry, struggling projects. Also, building a culture where helping others, showing empathy, and demonstrating compassion is both valued and noted will overcome this negative bias, especially in IT, where there is always more work than time. The toxicity of selfishness is always prevalent in dysfunctional organizations, not in emotionally healthy ones.

Empathy and Compassion: A Research Perspective

Compassion, that's the one thing no machine ever had. Maybe it's the one thing that keeps man ahead of them.

—**D. C. Fontana**

Most of the research into empathy and compassion concerns pain and suffering, two words rarely heard in corporations. It is more typical to speak about stress and a lack of work–life balance, but many toxic, antisocial behaviors can cause real pain and suffering for the victims. The victims of bullying, ostracism, deceit, and other toxic behaviors are real, and their pain is apparent. It is an unfortunate part of life in corporate America today. The degree to which these behaviors exist and are either tolerated or encouraged varies greatly from company to company.

There are many forms of suffering, some generated at the office and some brought to work. Most people have witnessed examples like these from within the office:

- A person works hard to achieve great results and then gets passed over for a promotion, especially when coworkers feel the decision was unfair.
- A poor review, delivered by a weak manager who has withheld his or her true sentiments all year, and then dumps a raft of negatives on an unsuspecting employee.
- The loss of good friends to layoffs, with their attendant pain and suffering.

Others sources of suffering occur outside of work, such as sick family members, the loss of an elder, problems with a child, monetary issues, marital issues, and many others that are emotional burdens that lessen the cognitive effectiveness of the individuals impacted.

Although there is pain, one finds thoughtful, compassionate individuals in corporations who support the suffering so that they don't feel alone. In addition, when someone helps another person, the strength of the bond between the two individuals increases, providing lasting and improved social cohesion. If replicated through many simple acts, it can have a large, positive effect on the emotional health and functioning of the organization.

At an organizational level, researchers characterize compassion into the subprocesses of "noticing, feeling and responding, each contributing uniquely to the process of compassion."[6] Furthermore, these same researchers go on to state that "by strengthening people's feelings of connectedness, the process of compassion builds and shapes the communities in which we live and work."[7] This is precisely what I have witnessed, as mood and productivity are positively elevated when workers care for one another.

Both individual and organizational compassion exist. From an organizational perspective, compassion functions when "members of a system collectively notice, feel and respond to pain experienced by members of that system. . . . [T]hese sub-processes become collective when they are legitimated within an organizational context and propagated among organizational members."[8]

Looking at the three subprocesses reveals how they operate. Anyone tuned in to their work environment has witnessed or used all three. The first is the capability to *notice* a coworker or subordinate's painful or unhappy mood. It was always very clear to me when an individual's mood had negatively shifted. Being sincerely concerned, I would say something like "You don't look happy. What's up?" The positive reaction was immediate, and the mere fact that the chief information officer noticed had an ameliorative impact. Some of the burden was lessened, and people were better able to get back to work, knowing I cared.

Next there is *feeling*. People who have compassion can actually feel another's pain through their mirror neurons, a powerful source of connectedness. In fact, if you look up where the word *compassion* comes from, you will find it has a Latin root meaning to suffer along with someone else and feel pity for them. The exact definition of *compassion* is "the ability for a person to feel what the other person is feeling (sometimes considered empathy or even sympathy). Yet more so, we see in the word compassion the ability for a person to fully feel the emotional grief and suffering of another with them in the present moment."[9]

Last, there is the most important process: *responding*. As Sogyal Rinpoche (1992) explains, compassion "is not simply a sense of sympathy or caring for the person suffering, not simply a warmth of heart toward the person before you, or a sharp recognition of their needs and pain, it is also a sustained and practical determination to do whatever is possible and necessary to help alleviate their suffering."[10]

For empathy and compassion to work at an organizational level, they need to become part of the social fabric, with visible actions that make it okay to care about others. There are good examples that any manager can adapt to their own organization. Consider Cisco Systems, cited as an example in 2004, which offers an example of an organization with policies that create such a capacity:

> "John Chambers, CEO, has a policy that he is to be notified (within 48 hours) of every instance in which a Cisco employee or an employee's immediate family member falls seriously ill or passes away. This policy increases individual members' vigilance by encouraging them to be on the lookout for pain."[11]

By making the sub-processes of noticing, feeling, and responding organizational imperatives, management can facilitate organizational compassion at all levels of the enterprise. It is simply a matter of awareness, priority, and modeling the right behavior. If management does model this behavior, it has enormous impact because humans are highly aware of social hierarchy and are most likely to model the behavior of their superiors. Whatever energy is expended on compassion is paid back multiple times in productivity gains from employees who feel needed, cared about, and safe and therefore are more relaxed and able to dive into their cognitive responsibilities.

It is up to management to wisely use compassion as a driver of improved mood for the organization. Compassion is a form of potential energy waiting to be unlocked. Now that I have firmly laid out the emotions of empathy and compassion as management tools, let's look deeply into how caring behaviors lead to deeply collaborative work environments, which I refer to as Collaborative Social Systems.

Notes

1. P. Frost and S. Robinson, "The Toxic Handler: Organizational Hero—and Casualty," *Harvard Business Review* (July-August 1999, 97–106. You can also visit hbr.org and find a lot of valuable research, and this article.
2. Ibid., 98.
3. Ibid.
4. Ibid., 100.
5. John M. Darley and C. Daniel Batson, "From Jerusalem to Jericho: A Study of Situational and Dispositional Variables in Helping Behavior," 1973. Available at www.aug.edu/sociology/Jerusalem.htm.
6. Jason M. Kanov, Sally Maitlis, Monica C. Worline, Jane E. Dutton, Peter J. Frost, and Jacoba M. Lilius, "Compassion in Organizational Life," *American Behavioral Scientist* 47 (2004): 808–827. Available at webuser.bus.umich.edu/janedut/Compassion/Comp%20Organ%20Life.pdf.
7. Ibid., 809.
8. Ibid., 810.
9. Ucadia.org, definition of *compassion*. Available at www.ucadia.com/concepts_emotions/concept_emotions_pos_compassion.htm.
10. Kanov et al., "Compassion in Organizational Life," 813–814.
11. Ibid., 817.

CHAPTER 8

Designing a Collaborative Social System

Working Social: How the Right Culture Unlocks Productivity

The fact is, culture eats strategy for lunch. You can have a good strategy in place, but if don't have the culture and the enabling systems that allow you to successfully implement that strategy, the culture of the organization will defeat the strategy.

—DICK CLARK, FORMER CEO, MERCK

In information technology (IT), a social system is not just a sociological term but the actual means of production. Our industrial-era command-and-control structure of departments and divisions established a formal hierarchy that has become the accepted way to view an organization. But other hierarchies drive the pace of work, both formal and informal, including ad hoc teams, cross-functional units, structured interaction with third-party partners, as well as the social hierarchy, which is different from the formal one. These hierarchies shift and move as projects and teams evolve. All of these structures work only if there is open and meaningful collaboration. Collaboration is a vital ingredient for project success, so every manager must build a *collaborative social system* where collaboration occurs throughout the social environment. It is a key to unlocking potential.

"Collaboration is a process through which people who see different aspects of a problem can constructively explore their differences and search for solutions that go beyond their own limited vision of what is possible."[1]

At work, management never talks about the social environment but prefers to use the word *culture*. The notion of a social system is a foreign concept, but it is real, and the rise of social network technology is bringing this notion into the mainstream. Moreover, humans are social animals and are wired for social interaction, so it is a fundamental aspect of organizational life.

Personally, IT is all about *working social*. Yes, there is a culture, which is the shared beliefs and behaviors, but within the organizational structure you have many social systems, woven together (or not) with boundaries that are rarely seamless. The social dimensions, such as social interaction, social climate, social connectedness, social collaboration, social intelligence, and so on, are the foundations of shared outcomes.

As noted before, IT is a product of many minds and emotions, knitted together such that the whole is significantly greater than the sum of the parts. Very little value is generated by an individual working alone. People are always part of a team, and more broadly, many parts of the organization contribute to success. The more deeply they are sharing, working together, and pulling in one direction, the better the outcome. Without collaboration, IT literally cannot function. You fail before you start.

As people initially collaborate, they do so based on the cultural values and beliefs within their social environment that have been either communicated and embraced or observed and copied. How well they gel depends on whether the social chemistry is positive or negative. Since they share work, behavior, and beliefs, they begin to identify with one another, interpersonal bonds form, and interaction deepens. Solidarity grows, and the social system takes shape—a disparate and disconnected group of individuals now united.

Everyone in IT needs to work together to unlock the social drivers of success so that the company, management, and employees all thrive. This is every worker's responsibility, whether you are the chief information officer, a leader within the organization, or an individual contributor. Each individual works within a social structure, and how well people do this determines the collective success or failure of projects as well as individual careers. Overlook this at your own peril.

Designing Collaborative Social Systems

Over many years and many turnarounds, I found a formula that powerfully unlocks the productivity potential of a social system. In order to build a social environment that is highly collaborative, you must build shared culture that allows a productive social fabric to form, one thread at a time. Yes, individuals become teams when the right culture exists. Behavior reinforces cultural norms, and in Chapter 9 we look at how you share productive behavior, but for now, let's focus on the cultural constructs.

People always want to understand the difference between teamwork and collaboration. Simply put, it is one of scale. Teams are small groups of tightly knit individuals connected by their daily responsibilities, while collaboration is the means by which the entire company/organization works together, extending even to partners. Collaboration connects teams, social units, social systems, and ultimately the social complex—a division: the largest building block of a modern company (unless it is a holding company with many subsidiaries).

Based on my role, I have operated at different levels across companies during my career. I always strove to achieve healthy collaboration and succeeded within the limitations of the overarching culture. The broader culture has an enormous impact because the need to collaborate extends beyond IT's management boundaries. You can build and shape your own social environment, but the enterprise takes over beyond that. Yes, you can have an influence over the "whole" based on your peer relationships and how well you engage them in the need to collaborate. That said, your control is indirect, through influence, so it is less powerful as you are not part of that social hierarchy.

Even if collaboration is listed as an *organizational competency* by Human Resources, unless all senior executives embrace it, reinforce it by what they say, and, most important, how they act, it remains a goal, not a reality. How people actually behave influences the culture around them and shapes the culture below them. Tone at "the top" is very powerful. Setting clear goals for how the social system will operate is critical.

COLLABORATIVE SOCIAL SYSTEM

A collection of individuals with deeply trusting relationships, operating within a caring and supportive culture where interaction is frictionless, and where members behave unselfishly by focusing on the needs of others and their organization, over their own.

To turn your culture into a collaborative social system, try instilling the following human factors throughout your organization or team. Here is your speech:

I am so proud of you. We are a remarkable organization, filled with incredible talent that will reach great heights to the benefit of every team member. Our social system is the loom upon which we all weave a fabric of great strength, resilience, and productivity. Each of you is an important piece of this amazing organizational tapestry, and today I want to share a vision of how we will emotionally unite everyone, creating a social fabric that will enable us to outperform, outdeliver, and outcreate the competition.

Our tapestry is sewn in the image of a *collaborative social system*, where each thread is held tightly together because we:

1. **Trust one another and the organization**. Trust must be fully operational here. We need to ensure it exists at three levels, as defined by Galford and Drapeau: *organizational, interpersonal,* and *strategic*.[2] These represent the competence of the management team to lead the company—strategic; a culture where people behave in others' best interest—interpersonal; and organizational processes like compensation and promotions, to name a couple, that are fair and garner the trust of the employees—organizational. For IT, we must take the academic notion of interpersonal trust further, because it needs to exist between every member of our extended organization; otherwise portions of our fabric will unravel.

    Depending on where you operate in the company, you can influence one or all of these levels. For each of you, I ask that you build interpersonal trust, as it is the vital thread of our collaborative social system. When levels of trust flow deeply between individuals, it drives organizational effectiveness; things begin to flow; understanding opens up, and distrust, a form of friction, is minimized so it doesn't impinge on our work.

    As a leader, you must help us build all three. [The chief executive can have the greatest influence on all three, but even at the level of a division (social complex) or department (social system), a leader can rally the team, design fair and unbureaucratic processes, and focus on doing the right things.] As always, trust at an individual level comes down to being authentic, honoring your commitments, being a team player, and doing the right things. What is right is situational, but for most of you this needs no explanation. Right and wrong are normally obvious, especially if each of you focuses on the needs of others, not your own. Being unselfish will do more to build interpersonal trust than just about anything. George Manning, professor of business at Northern Kentucky University, says, "Managers who lie betray the trust and respect of their staff. Without trust and respect, an institution will fail. It's the glue that binds people together."[3]

2. **Are highly collaborative**. Collaboration by itself isn't enough. We need to go beyond basic collaboration, reaching a point where our interaction is effortless because we are so tightly bound to one another and our mission. This doesn't mean we don't disagree or express our opinion—we do, because each member's thoughts are valued, and everyone's voice must be heard. But our levels of trust

and caring for one another must reach a level where team members do not have to engage in protective behaviors and work flows freely between us. Our success will be characterized by the lack of *social friction* in our interactions. We will have moved beyond individual *states of flow*, to one where we are in a *state of flow together*. The inhibition and social friction will be gone, and our organization will be free to pick up speed, achieving high levels of productivity and creativity, a true competitive threat to those we face in the marketplace. This is about winning. Let all of our energy be invested in competitive advantage, not antisocial and protective behaviors.

3. **Are caring**. Everyone here needs to care about each other [refer back to empathy and compassion in Chapter 7], our work quality, and exceeding expectations. If we don't care, then we are behaving self-ishly, and this is a cancer that will eat away at the connective tissue of our area. Selfish organizations and individuals are destined to fail, as the *corporate immune system*, and the marketplace, will ultimately exact full retribution. Yes, short-term capital gains are possible, including bigger raises and promotions because an individual has taken advantage of others to garner extra credit or recognition. Longer term, it was undeserved, and the truth will come out by means of the grapevine, or a poor follow-on performance. We must create an environment where everyone—leader, individual contributor, star—all model this behavior so it infectiously permeates our social chemistry. Anything less is both a collective failure and a failure of management.

4. **Act with candor, openness, and respect**. IT is highly specialized. We each bring skills, but let us all recognize that there are many forms of intelligence so we must humbly be open to others ideas. For instance, some of you may be great communicators and others not at all. As a team, we are *respectful* of others and accept each team member for what and who they are. If they can't communicate well and stumble presenting an idea, we patiently wait for them to share their thoughts and show our patience by not cutting them off. This is just one example of the tolerance and respect we must have for one another in everything we do. Every team member is accepted for who they are, because we succeed or fail as a team. Encourage others to contribute (speak up), be *open* to their ideas, and accept them so they find comfort as part of our organization. Candor is of great value especially because we are an *active listening social system*.

5. **Strive for harmony**. One sign that we have achieved our goal is a feeling of personal and group harmony. When we are collaborating deeply and there is mutual respect, acceptance, and joy, then harmony can be felt. It feels good and increases the emotional energy level of

our area. According to the *World English Dictionary* (available online at Dictionary.com), *harmony* is "agreement in action, opinion, feeling, etc.; accord." But because we are open and encourage candor, harmony does not represent an absence of conflict: "The absence of conflict is not harmony; it's apathy."[4]

6. **Operate transparently.** To me, transparency is indispensable to success. When you have complete transparency, there are no hidden agendas to fear, and the intent is known—good or bad. We all know that not everything that happens is good—that's life. So both good and bad will be shared. Knowing this, everyone on our team can relax, because they are fully informed. Never withhold information from others for personal or organizational reasons. Hidden agendas create subtle forms of friction as people waste precious mental cycles trying to read intent into everything. It is hard to relax and achieve a state of flow if you are never sure what might hurt you. Such environments are toxic. We must not leave people in the dark, by design or by accident.

7. **Share freely and help one another.** As I have said many times, success is social. In IT, as you know, many minds produce one result. So, sharing information and helping other team members is vitally important. Unfortunately, a common personal survival tactic among workers in unhealthy organizations is withholding knowledge that fellow team members need to prosper, so you can look better than them. In fact, when one team member fails we all are impacted, as ours is a group outcome.

   In addition, IT is highly specialized, so sharing and teamwork are imperative for productivity. At a personal level, you will not achieve power or security by keeping information to yourself; you will only corrode group success. Since we care about one another, do your best, yet share information freely so that everyone has all the information they need to succeed and be their best.

8. **Operate without blame.** I've often wondered how helpful and instructive it would be if you could calculate the return on investment (ROI) of *zero blame*, for, as Oscar Wilde said, "Experience is the name everyone gives to their mistakes." As we learn, we all make mistakes; it is an indispensable part of growing institutional knowledge. At the moment, we don't have enough data and understanding to calculate such an ROI, but it is significant. Having taken over organizations where blame was prevalent, I can tell you with certainty that it is highly corrosive.

   For those of us who have been able to transform an organization, we have seen blame destroy individual mood and lower emotional energy levels and, with it, group productivity. As Einstein said, "Not everything that counts can be measured. And not everything that can be measured counts." So, we can't measure productivity, but we don't have to. Errors are just mistakes, and we encourage people to try and fail rather than never try at all. That said, repeated mistakes are errors. Those are not acceptable.

9. **Are proactive.** This is a safe environment, so please feel comfortable taking initiative. I expect everyone to autonomously look for ways to improve environments, systems, our culture, relationships with coworkers, and anything else that can be improved. People shouldn't wait for an issue to pop up and then react to correct it. We can overcome anything if each of us leaves work each day thinking about how we can make this a better place, with better solutions and happier customers. Thousands of little improvements create giant steps forward. Let's take these steps together, united by our action.

10. **Are unselfish.** Kindness is contagious, because people don't do what you say; they model their behavior based on what those around them do. This is true whether you are the manager or an individual contributor, but managers have the most impact because humans are very sensitive to the social hierarchy. It's just the way it is. My personal theory is that, as we evolved, speech came much later than our social nature. (This isn't a fact, just my belief.) Most learning was therefore observational; if not, as a species, we would have ceased to exist because children could not learn behaviors. Long before they learn to speak, children copy what those around them do. Behavior is a very important means of transmitting group norms.

Why a Collaborative Social System Matters

Leaders get into everyone's skin, exuding positive energy and optimism. Unhappy tribes have a tough time winning.

—JACK WELCH

When you create a culture with the characteristics discussed in this chapter, the social sentiment is happy, motivated, upbeat, and highly productive, with a high degree of social cohesion (deep and enduring trust) and freely flowing information. Remember, your culture is a *creative cocoon*—it envelops the people and is either supportive or detrimental to productivity. The culture is shared, so everyone must take a hand in shaping it. That is why you must engage every individual to be personally responsible for shaping the collaborative social system and accelerating its evolution. At that point, you have created a high-trust environment, characterized by a positive, upbeat mood, where productivity flows unencumbered by dark emotions and protective behavior.

A healthy and productive culture is the result of wise cultural design decisions. To make wise choices it is important to understand the "equipment" you use. In the emotional midbrain, our limbic system, over 90 percent of the wiring is for survival, driving how we respond to threats/fear. This makes sense since survival is the key function of any organism, so that it can reproduce and its genes can continue. How else would we have gotten here? We are in fact masters of survival.

The goal of a collaborative social system is therefore to eliminate fear and the protective behaviors it creates and to avoid the cognitively debilitating effects created when the limbic system impedes higher thought to focus energy and action on survival (see Chapter 6). The cliché *bad chemistry* is nothing more than a social environment where toxic and untrustworthy behaviors predominate and fear is evident. By eliminating fear and the behaviors that get in the way of trust, people become connected, and the degree of connectedness drives the exchange of information that is so important to getting everyone on the same page, through shared understanding. This is a critical productivity lever because healthy, strong bonds bring forth high-quality output; if these bonds don't exist, productive energy is silently consumed in countless strained connections (social friction), and disappointing results are the final outcome.

You can think of it this way: The social environment drives the speed and success of collaboration among your co-creators. It is the crucible into which all of the human ingredients—collective aptitude, EQ, experience, and IQ—are poured and within which the group creative process—commonly known as projects—takes place. It has its own ambience based on the mixture of people involved.

Leaders shape this environment to increase its effectiveness, much like an artist chisels a sculpture out of a difficult material and unlocks the beauty hidden within. Productively shaping social output by building a cohesive and high-aptitude culture requires outward focus, social insight, extroverted sensitivity, and a caring, unselfish orientation. It is an art rather than a science, but today this social environment remains concealed within the industrial-era concept of *organization*.

But today, unlike during the industrial era, the human infrastructure has to be socially cohesive, engaged, upbeat, collaborative, and supported by a healthy social climate; this matters much more than the structure and processes, because we already have competence in those areas. If the human factors are poorly shaped, a weak performance and/or failure are inevitable; if they are designed right, you have a foundation for success.

Chapter 11 is devoted solely to social and emotional intelligence. It influences every dollar invested, the return on every interaction, and the ultimate outcome of the project. Both are used to shape the emotional climate, rules of engagement, and so on that support the intense collaboration required to build something that cannot be physically seen, touched, or felt other than around the edges (the user interface, reports, etc.). It is more important than the selection of any tool or the addition of any individual. This is about organizational potential: the array of subtle factors that govern the quality of the outcome and its ROI. The ultimate return is governed by many factors external to IT, such as the quality of the business strategy and marketing effectiveness, but within IT, the emotional climate is a vital productivity driver.

I have scanned the research, and there is more written about teamwork than collaboration. Collaboration isn't an academic focus, although perhaps it will become one. That said, relevant research in this area proves what anyone who directs departments of people has discovered on their own: Working together is fundamental.

For instance, Wenpin Tsai studied how social capital leads to improved knowledge sharing. Professionals who are trustworthy and help others, build strong social capital for themselves and are able to get things done using their connections. "Social capital represents the relational resources attainable by individual actors through networks of social relationships."[5] Tsai goes on to quote other researchers who state that "an actor's trustworthiness signals to other parties (including both those that have interacted with the actor in the past, and those that have not) its willingness to forego [sic] short-term outcomes obtainable through opportunistic behaviors."[6] It is quite clear to anyone who has worked in a corporation that cunning, selfish behavior lowers group productivity by directing short-term gains to a single individual. This is highly corrosive, and destroys trust. Trust is a well-studied, pivotal lever of team effectiveness. You must demand it.

Another study distinguished internal conflict among the information systems project team from the conflict of project team members with external users. Both internal and external team conflicts are found to impact interaction quality negatively, which in turn is strongly and positively related to project performance. These relationships indicate that attention to both internal and external conflict is crucial in achieving project goals.[7] This is why harmony, across business and IT, is paramount. The deeper the harmony, the stronger and more real the interaction.

There is also no question from the research that you have to hire for collaboration and keep it alive in your culture; if not, collaboration becomes part of the written values but not the practices. I have seen this a number of times across companies, so living the values is more important than writing them down. The research has found this as well. As Lynda Gratton explains:

Despite the corporate rhetoric of cooperation and teamwork, unwritten rules encouraged people to outshine everyone around them. Rather than sharing ideas and know-how, people hoarded knowledge and worked with others as little as possible. Within weeks of joining the company, new hires learned to talk up cooperation, while acting competitively. In this company . . . a gap exists between the rhetoric of creative cooperating and the reality of unproductive competition.[8]

I can't reinforce enough the need for open sharing. It is an indispensable behavior that has unlocked much collective intelligence that I have then put to use in large programs across companies. Key players often have valuable insights that must be shared to maximize their value and help other team members avoid bad decisions. Helping others builds social capital and increases interpersonal trust, as shown in a study where "the processes and actions encompassed by the attitudes toward and the behavior of 'sharing' is the major factor influencing collaborative team trust building."[9] This isn't just opinion; it is a fact that should be leveraged to improve success ratios.

You can achieve a lot by modeling all of these values and overarching cultural goals. But you can really make a collaborative culture operate powerfully by defining a model for behavior. Much has been written about organizational citizenship behavior, so let's take a look at that in detail in Chapter 9.

Notes

1. Shawn Callahan, Mark Schenk, and Nancy White, "Building a Collaborative Workplace," April 2008. Available at www.anecdote.com.au/whitepapers.php?wpid=15.
2. Robert Galford and Anne S. Drapeau, "The Enemies of Trust," *Harvard Business Review* (February 2003). Available at http://hbr.org/2003/02/the-enemies-of-trust/ar/1.
3. Bill Wolfe, "Caring Leadership Lives, Author Contends. Not Everybody's Been a Jerk, Kentuckian Says," *Courier-Journal*, September 22, 2002. Available at www.nku.edu/~manningg/cjleader.html.
4. Kathleen M. Eisenhardt, Jean L. Kahwajy, and L. J. Bourgeois III, "How Management Teams Can Have a Good Fight," *Harvard Business Review* (July-August 1997): 77. Available at http://wweb.uta.edu/management/lavelle/New%20Folder/HowManagementTeamsCanFight.pdf.
5. Wenpin Tsai, "Social Capital, Strategic Relatedness and the Formation of Intraorganizational Linkages," *Strategic Management Journal* 21(9): 927. Available at www.jstor.org/discover/10.2307/3094261?uid=2&uid=4&sid=21101368592147.
6. Ibid.
7. Eric T. G. Wang, Henry H. G. Chen, James J. Jiang, and Gary Klein, "Interaction Quality Between IS Professionals and Users: Impacting Conflict and Project Performance," *Journal of Information Science* 31, no. 4 (2005): 280.
8. Lynda Gratton, "How to Foster a Cooperative Culture," HBR Blog Network/Best Practices, January 15, 2009. Available at http://blogs.hbr.org/hmu/2009/01/four-ways-to-encourage-more-pr.html.
9. Valerie Lynne Herzog, "Trust Building on Corporate Collaborative Project Teams," *Project Management Journal* (March 2001): 30.

CHAPTER 9

The Social Compact

Organizational Citizenship Behavior

Let people realize clearly that every time they threaten someone or humiliate or unnecessarily hurt or dominate or reject another human being, they become forces for the creation of psychopathology, even if these be small forces. Let them recognize that every person who is kind, helpful, decent, psychologically democratic, affectionate, and warm, is a psychotheraputic force, even though a small one.

—ABRAHAM MASLOW

Information technology (IT) is all about behavior—prosocial behavior. I have turned around many organizations that failed because of socially toxic leadership. Based on my experience, nothing influences productivity and organizational effectiveness more than behavior when groups of individuals have to collaborate to accomplish something. You can promote the mission and try to spread the culture, but what gets acted out broadly across a division or narrowly in isolated pockets, becomes the social norm. This behavior can range from horribly antisocial, to warmly prosocial, or anything in between. What's true is that inconsistency is the rule. It needn't be.

Of course, I have seen great variation in behavior across divisions and departments, regardless of the corporate values. My experience is that the workers were always socially sensitive to the power hierarchy, so what they said, and how they acted, was determined mostly by the *tone at the top* of their local organization. In a social system, understanding and adapting to unwritten behavioral norms is a basic survival skill. The loudest tone normally comes from the immediate management who control the workers' survival. When the values and messages from senior management are very different from those transmitted locally, the tone from senior management is barely heard if behavioral norms are not enforced by filtering out leaders who get good results but exact a high human price (unless of course that *is* the culture).

What exactly is "tone at the top"? To me, it is a combination of behavior and communication. If both are aligned, they are a powerful mix. But when words and deeds are at odds, leadership behavior sets the tone. Everyone talks about corporate culture, but most of the time culture and behavior vary markedly, because behavioral norms are rarely enforced. Unfortunately, in such cases, a critical lever of productivity is open to local variation.

Living the Values

Companies normally talk about culture, instead of tone and behavior, and oftentimes write glowingly about how strong theirs is. It is very important, but unfortunately it varies greatly from division to division in most companies. Culture establishes a set of values that should be consistently embraced. As a matter of fact, shared and enduring values have been shown to be critical drivers that separate lasting enterprises from those that fail. Consequently, "living the values" is what really matters. Sadly, in many companies, values are no more than a sign on the wall or a highlight in the annual report. As noted here and in Chapter 8, the collective behavior of the executives and middle management is what actually gets embraced. Those are the *true values*. Everyone sees them and emulates them; they become the macro- and microcultures.

One lives the values by modeling them in daily business interactions, talking about what they mean at town hall meetings, and sharing stories where the values made a difference. By doing so, their power and importance are consistently reinforced. Although modeling them is effective, a consistent culture can only exist when everyone shares a common understanding of what living them actually means. In an IT organization that is highly dependent on collaboration, it isn't enough to just say "We collaborate and help one another"; no, guidelines for effective collaboration need to be unambiguously described. That ensures people understand not just the words, but their very essence.

To achieve this, I recommend leaders engage their organization to define written guidelines, in collaboration with human resources, that explicitly describe the behaviors that are productive, and why they are productive. Doing this ensures management and the employees both understand what living them means. Having written guidelines endorsed by the community empowers people to point out "unacceptable" behavior, which is an important, real-time governor that improves collaboration at the point of interaction.

This self-reinforcing cycle of correction provides an ongoing productivity dividend that goes right to the bottom line. The productivity is already there; it just needs to be unlocked.

In academia, the notion of behavior and how it impacts organizational effectiveness is a mature area of research. Dennis Organ, who retired from the University of Indiana, and Thomas Bateman, from the University of Texas, are credited with founding this area, which is called organizational citizenship behavior (OCB). They first wrote about OCB in 1983 and defined it as "those organizationally beneficial behaviors and gestures that can neither be enforced on the basis of formal role obligations nor elicited by contractual guarantee of recompense."[1]

Under the constructs of OCB, behaviors include everything that improves job performance and the performance of the organization that are not specifically related to getting the task done. So, if an employee has been assigned to write a program (the task), yet also helps others by answering questions, sharing information freely, and showing empathy and concern, these are examples of what OCB is. An individual who cares deeply about the mission and coworkers, who goes the extra mile, and works hard to help others and the organization succeed is exhibiting OCB. Such people are prosocial and empathetic, behaving in a genuinely caring way, motivated to get the job done, and not exhibiting negative behaviors. Their behavior is precisely what you want to amplify across your organization.

In 1988, Organ redefined OCB as "individual behavior that is discretionary, not directly or explicitly recognized by the formal reward system, and that in the aggregate promotes the effective functioning of the organization."[2] He went on to say that *discretionary* refers "to behaviors that are not ambiguously required by the role, and are therefore done voluntarily in order to help the team and greater organization succeed." I wrote about the research on OCB in Chapter 6, so refer back to that for more detail.

However, by 1988, the world of work was changing. When Organ first began his organizational psychology research, jobs were very well defined, with specific roles and explicit duties. As we moved from an industrial to an information economy, job expectations changed. In knowledge work, much of what we do involves problem solving, designing, creating, and collectively adding value. The role has a clear objective, but there is more individual control over what gets delivered and how it is delivered. As noted by Organ, Borman and Motowidlo redefined OCB as "behaviors that do not support the technical core itself so much as they support the broader organizational, social, and psychological environment."[3] I think this definition accurately describes the social environment and chemistry that govern knowledge worker productivity in IT.

Shaping IT: One Interaction at a Time

It is very clear—and I agree, based on my experience—ensuring the social environment and the collective mood and psychology are positive is what matters. Then people behave productively in their interpersonal interactions and statements, engendering a warm, caring and supportive environment that infuses their job as well. Overall, the speed and quality of interaction is paramount. IT happens because thousands of peer-to-peer, manager-to-manager, and manager-to-subordinate interactions that take place all day, every working day. These interactions shape employees' perceptions and morale, so nothing could be more important than molding interpersonal behavior.

To me, interpersonal behavior is a critical element of success—it is ultimately how the human factory runs. If you have an assembly line with detailed process manuals but the machines are incorrectly programmed and therefore can't pass the material between them, yield drops. Things are no different in a collaborative social system. You can post the word *collaborate* everywhere, but if management models uncollaborative behavior, the workers will become uncollaborative *because management unknowingly programmed them that way.* Managers wouldn't allow such a situation to persist on an assembly line, but, in the case of knowledge work, we accept it every day across traditional corporate America.

For the record, prosocial behavior isn't a panacea, just an important element of organizational success. It doesn't eliminate the need for the right strategy or any of the other disciplines that drive organizational effectiveness. But with the right behaviors, you have the best chance of turning great strategy into enduring success. If you have built a collaborative social system, work flows freely and the values penetrate deeply into the psyche and behavior of the organization.

Since Organ, some academics have taken the notion of OCB further, by recognizing how critical the role of management is in establishing behavioral norms. This research looks into *management citizenship behavior*, and in my experience, it is more important than OCB. Members of management establish the culture through their *living values*. When cultures fail, it is a failure of management—nothing else. Employees have the utmost sensitivity to the social hierarchy and pick up what the top people are doing.

Behavior drives broad organizational effectiveness. As noted earlier, you should go further than modeling the right behavior by establishing clear guidelines that approach policy but aren't that restrictive. Don't make the mistake of "bringing the behaviors down from the mountain" and issuing a behavioral policy manual—overcontrol is always unproductive in knowledge work. No, it is far better to engage the entire organization by forming a group of volunteers to own and drive the guidelines for productive collaboration. Membership in this group should rotate, to engage a cross-section of the employee base. With this representative body, employees retain control of their interaction model, and control is a consistent driver of higher engagement and productivity.

What I am recommending is similar to customer service where workers are trained to politely and effectively interact with clients: how to greet them, how to remain calm, how to listen, how to be respectful, how to ensure the customer feels you have their best interest in mind. In customer service, what you do and say matters immensely. As the head of Client Services at a major brokerage firm, I saw firsthand how important this training was to our mission to deliver consistent, high-quality service and build customer intimacy. In IT, understanding how to work productively with co-creators is an element of professional intimacy, and it is equally important.

IT is highly collaborative. What individuals do and say has an enormous impact on the social dynamic and whether it is productive or unproductive. But unlike customer service, where clients can call back and get a different representative if they don't like who answered the phone, inside the company, you must interact with certain coworkers. That is why prosocial behavior is critical. You build a successful IT organization one interaction at a time. Make no mistake about it, *we are in the interaction era*.

Courtesy Is Contagious

If you judge people, you have no time to love them.

—Mother Teresa

Successful social systems have a bias that is outwardly focused on group needs rather than individual ones. This is not to suggest that you cannot meet your needs and get your work done; you must. But doing that is only part of the job. The balance of your time is spent helping the IT orchestra create great music.

Social etiquette is a lubricant that accelerates cooperative work through mutual respect. To quote Organ: "Courtesy can perform wonders for the flow and scheduling of interdependent work activities, not to mention the preservation of emotional stamina among many parties for constructive contributions rather than verbal disputes."[4] The behavioral guidelines listed on the following pages include some basic etiquette (courtesy) and are designed to help orient the group toward sharing and concern for one another. The goal is to subordinate the concept of self beneath the group's needs and shift the bias from selfish to unselfish. This is the foundation of a *social compact* that will help individuals balance group versus individual needs.

Unfortunately, social etiquette has fallen out of favor and is now almost forgotten. A number of etiquette books were still in use when I was growing up, and I remember having proper manners reinforced at home as a child. Not that long ago, manners/etiquette were an important part of social conduct, but their use was rejected by a generation that found them unhip and stuffy. Yet these social rituals are an important means of showing respect for one another, especially in a system where each person's success is dependent on the social group. Etiquette represents an important, time-tested code of conduct that adds social value. Its use shows respect, and respect for one another builds trust. Trust is the lubricant that opens collaborative flow between individuals.

Leaders should model the use of etiquette by saying thank you, and opening the door for everyone, not just higher-ups where the intent is to kiss up. I went out of my way to interact respectfully with everyone, especially those subordinate to me, so they would understand I was not actually above them—I just had a higher position in the company. Putting the guidelines for effective collaboration into print, as suggested earlier, establishes a depersonalized basis for bringing unproductive behavior to the attention of coworkers who cause friction or are disrespectful. Viewing IT as an orchestra, etiquette is a social lubricant that opens connections between members, shaping a productive environment in which composers share mutual respect and understanding. Joint composition is, after all, possible only when people respect one another.

The next 40 behavioral guidelines are very simple and productivity enhancing. Remember, courtesy, like all behaviors, is contagious. This list is not specific to any organization, just examples you can use to stimulate conversation among the volunteers working on your guidelines. As I said earlier, engage your organization and create your own. Remember, "OCB includes not only enactment of positive gestures and contributions, but also the quality of forbearance—the willingness to endure the occasional costs, inconveniences, and minor frustrations attendant to collective endeavors."[5]

1. **Listen attentively; do not interrupt**. This guideline is believed by many but practiced by few. In a social environment where trust is the critical lubricant, stopping someone from sharing their thoughts and insights is disrespectful and unproductive. People want to add value. Preventing them from doing this creates resentment because you have failed to let them contribute. Impatiently cutting people off sends a message that you are faster (I know what you are going to say before you say it), smarter (I will give you the word you are groping for), and uncollaborative. Many people struggle with this, including me. Patient listening requires discipline and reinforcement.

   By listening intently, you send an unambiguous message that you, the listener, value what your coworker has to say; you respect the fact that their expression relies on a train of thought, and interrupting them causes thoughts to be lost and dialogue to be broken. So, although it feels efficient to speed things along, doing so slows progress down and limits the ability to form an emotional connection with someone. The conversation is one piece of the value, and the fact you care enough to listen is the other. Net net, listening is a key indicator of the level of respect between individuals within the social system.

2. **Use e-mail/messages for communication, not politics**. Your coworkers are far too busy to sift through burdensome amounts of e-mail/messages that have limited value. A contributing factor to the volume is people's desire to protect themselves (a not-so-hidden agenda) by copying everyone, turning e-mail into political cover (a notion that is visible to the team). The consequences are twofold: lost time and distrust, both of which are destructive and counterproductive behaviors. Out of respect for everyone, e-mail/messages must be used on a *need-to-know* basis, unless you are distributing documentation or reference material, which should be labeled as such. Since every successful social system is collaborative in nature, members are obliged to forward mail on to someone that was erroneously not copied. In this fashion, those that need to know will know.

3. **Do not raise issues without first speaking with the owner**. Something is not an issue unless you have discussed it with the owner, and he or she reports it, or is warned that you are going to raise it if the person will not. Blindsiding individuals by publicly raising issues you haven't spoken to them about destroys trust and teamwork. Reach out, make the connection, and discuss your concerns. Going to the issue owner one on one, shows you are sensitive to others' needs and are willing to collaborate productively with your coworkers.

4. **Keep all agendas public**. Hidden agendas are a social taboo. Team members should send a clear message that this type of destructive behavior is not acceptable for those wishing to be on the team.

5. **Share freely and often**. Everyone within the community needs to provide help and support to those around them. When everyone helps each another, the net impact accelerates the project. That said, requests for help need to be at socially acceptable thresholds that do not reach the level of *free riding*. When taking advantage is encountered, this needs to be dealt with, with tough love.

6. **Do not take advantage even if you can**. Taking advantage of someone who is very giving lessens one's character and is noticed by those nearby. The group needs to be clear that this is not allowed. When observed, it needs to be brought to the attention of the transgressor;

if not, the givers will share less freely, diminishing the organization's overall productivity.

7. **Avoid sidebar meetings**. Talking privately during a meeting is disruptive and unacceptable. Take your business off-line and do it at another time. The same goes for passing notes.

8. **Fully attend meetings**. It is an unfortunate sign of the times that people feel empowered to use mobile devices during meetings. (This criticism doesn't pertain to taking notes on a tablet.) This is thoroughly disrespectful. Everyone witnesses the behavior, and the message is clear: I have more important things to do than pay attention to your business. If you are too busy to be part of the meeting, respectfully bow out; if you really have a conflict, do not try to accomplish both at once because you will not.

   If you are responsible for the minutes, or the meeting requires a computer to participate, that is part of the accepted protocol. Please stay connected with those with whom you have a commitment, not someone who is interrupting the meeting from a distance.

9. **Be helpful**. Group success is a collaborative activity. No one can succeed alone on a project that requires integrating contributions from a diverse set of members. The orchestra requires a firm foundation of mutual support to achieve mutual success; when someone needs help, give it.

10. **Be truthful**. Honesty is a large-denomination currency. Provide candid, honest input. Rosy forecasts, oversimplifications, or spin, delays dealing with the truth—and the truth always comes out and must be dealt with. In an environment where honesty and candor are the policy, accurate input leads to better quality decisions. (People are much more willing to state the facts in blame-free social environments.)

11. **Respect social boundaries**. It is your responsibility to become familiar with the roles and responsibilities of the orchestra members. When you are considering a solution, if your design crosses over into someone else's area of responsibility, you must engage them. Do not violate social boundaries and ownership rules. Once someone is responsible for a portion of the work, you have the implied responsibility to *respect their ownership*, just as with private property. Make sure you understand the ownership landscape clearly. Respect social boundaries.

12. **Be honest about your capabilities**. Do not mislead the group. Significant time is lost because people overstate their level of experience and expertise. You have a responsibility to be realistic about your capabilities. The truth always comes out, and it is far less painful and damaging to have it come out in conversation ("I don't really know

that") rather than after time and resources are invested. This behavior is inconsiderate, wasteful, and undermines respect and cohesion while adding to the stress level of the group.

13. **Be appreciative and say thank you**. When someone helps you, take a minute and say thank you. If openness is not your style, drop them a brief note instead. Whatever your personal preference, be appreciative of those who have taken their time to help. The whole team reaps the benefit when helpfulness is positively reinforced and prevalent. Saying "thank you" helps knot the social fabric together, giving it strength and resilience.

14. **Be respectful**. Respect others for the value they can add. It is very easy to be critical, and doing so takes no talent. Finding the value in others is more difficult, so show that you understand their value by giving them respect when respect is due.

15. **Trust one another**. When you trust someone else by relying on them, you immediately form a bond with that individual. It is a form of respect and flattery to acknowledge someone else's value and contributions by having your success linked to theirs. Succeed together and build unity.

16. **Be sincere**. Have one face, not two. There is no compromising with this guideline. Insincerity is a highly corrosive force that needs to be dealt with head-on to avoid productivity losses.

17. **Honor your commitments**. If you can't do something, just say so; if you can, make it happen. The social fabric is composed of threads, and commitments are the ties that bind one to another. A missed commitment causes the fabric to unravel. Do what you say, and say what you will do.

18. **Give credit when credit is due**. Giving credit transmits positive energy among team members, so give credit freely. That said, do it sincerely, and when it is deserved. Giving credit when it is unwarranted is a transparent act that cheapens the individual offering the praise because it is insincere. If you don't mean it, the recipient will sense it and will feel diminished by the act, losing respect for you in the process.

19. **Take credit only when it is deserved**. In the same vein, do not take credit when it is not deserved. If a misunderstanding occurs, highlight the true owner, and make sure the credit is directed where it belongs. Doing this opens up connections among coworkers, builds trust, and increases people's willingness to share since everyone's intentions are honorable.

20. **Say "No, you first."** The conductor always holds the door for a member of the orchestra, no matter how new or junior. The conductor's

success depends on all of the composers/conductors under him or her. Treat them with respect and serve them. You will be rewarded with productivity and professionals who are motivated to do well.

21. **Point out unproductive behavior**. There needs to be a socially agreed on means of pointing out unproductive behavior. The leader must point out such behavior when it occurs in order to establish visible limits that cannot be crossed. Allowing people to publicly trample behavioral guidelines cheapens the rules and undermines the importance of social boundaries.

22. **Say "Thank you for bringing that to my attention."** Once a violation is pointed out, it is incumbent on the individual who violated the productivity guidelines to thank fellow orchestra members for bringing it to his or her attention. Doing this serves to publicly reinforce the shared importance of the social rules and, by doing so, strengthens the weave of the social fabric.

23. **Be direct**. When you make a statement, say what you mean. Do not make pacifying proclamations just to get beyond the immediate situation. Untrue statements are quickly identified, breed distrust, and break down social collaboration. Say what you mean and mean what you say.

24. **Do not put coworkers down**. If you have nothing good to say about a coworker, then don't say anything. Putting people down is not constructive, especially behind their backs. People who feel good about themselves and the social system they belong to will open up, relax, contribute, and add value. Their desire to produce is determined by their perception of whether who they are and what they do is appreciated. Building collaborative productivity is all about maximizing output across the group and creating a warm and inviting milieu where appreciation is fundamental to successfully releasing the group's potential.

25. **Pay attention even when no one is watching**. We have all heard the typing start up during a conference call. If you need to excuse yourself for a moment, do so. Otherwise, be there in mind and deed.

26. **Say "Excuse me."** If you need to barge into a meeting or a conversation, always say "Excuse me." You do not have the right, even if you have the authority, to rudely interrupt anyone. One individual is not better than another, and each member is dependent on the social system.

27. **Speak up and get help when needed**. Composers as well as conductors share each outcome. They have been given responsibility for certain things yet their accountability is to the social system (as granted by the company). When help is needed, it is the responsibility of the individual to ask for help because it is not one person's problem—it is everyone's. Delaying getting help until it is an emergency is a disservice to the team.

28. **Don't be self-aggrandizing.** It is rude to be self-aggrandizing. Do not tell everyone what great accomplishments you have achieved, who you know (name dropping), and how important you are/have been. Diverting others' eyes toward this halo of greatness leaves orchestra members wondering if you are trying to cover up incompetence; this suspicion distances people, making it more difficult to form bonds; and, beyond that, it repels people, increasing the gap between team members. Everyone is interdependent. Be humble and nonthreatening to others, and you will bond more easily.

29. **Don't talk behind someone's back.** If you have something that is worthwhile to share about a fellow member of the social system, say it to their face. If you are unwilling to discuss it with them, it is better left unsaid.

30. **Don't be verbally combative.** This behavior is totally unacceptable and destroys teamwork and communication. The conduct is so transparent that the conductor(s) should spot it immediately and address it. Allowing verbal combativeness is a signal that the creative environment is unhealthy and being poorly led.

31. **Don't share unhappiness.** Misery loves company. Unfortunately, in a collaborative social system, this type of sharing degrades the energy level of the group, lowering productivity. Although it may not be easy for some people, everyone must try to wear a happy face, sharing problems only in private moments with close friends. There is a physiological benefit to smiling in that it causes the release of neurotransmitters that make you feel better. Try it.

32. **Let go. Trust the group.** Everyone must embrace the notion that there is strength and success in unity. Do not overcontrol, as it is socially unacceptable to distrust your co-composers.

33. **Avoid feeble feedback.** Cowardly conductors sometimes hide behind other's private remarks—"So and so said . . .." This form of insincerity diminishes leaders unable (afraid) to deliver difficult messages (ergo the hiding). As a strategy it fails by short-circuiting the subject's receptivity and switching the focus to the person being quoted, not the issue at hand—the person never hears the feedback. Listeners recognize this ploy for what it is: unfair, spineless, and cheap. So, a comment made in private (itself questionable) now damages the bonds among *all three individuals*—a productivity-destroying outcome for sure. Any opportunity to modify the subject's behavior is lost while how "not to conduct" is perfectly modeled.

34. **Avoid condescension.** No matter what the situation, talking down to someone is absolutely forbidden. No matter how high up or how important you think you are, you should never destroy someone's

productive spirit by belittling them. This type of treatment builds resentment and creates reflexive contempt from the demeaned person, who will not hear you when you next interact because resentment will immediately come into his or her consciousness. In short, this behavior corrodes connections so they no longer work.

35. **Watch your tone of voice**. Always be aware of your tone of voice. People rarely perceive how they sound, because they are not trained to listen while they speak. Everyone can develop sensitivity to this at some level. Instead of just an inward or outward focus, be sensitive to how you sound and your expression. Your senses are a mirror, so use them.

36. **Say "I'm sorry."** Success is all about the social system, not the individual. If you examine how value is created, you find production occurs through meaningful codependence. Remember, *the social system is the factory*, everyone is responsible for its operation, and everyone is obligated to keep it running smoothly. When you violate a rule of etiquette, you weaken a social connection and, in so doing, slow the movement of information, lessening the quantity and quality of knowledge sharing. As a member of the system, you must act responsibly and say "I'm sorry."

   Job one is to ensure this factory, spun from human social fabric, operates full tilt through warm and open connections. Remember, saying you are sorry is a meaningful obligation that reopens and repairs damaged connections. Treat it that way, and all benefit. You, in fact, are the indirect beneficiary when other people patch up their differences. Keep connections open so that information flows unimpeded throughout the community.

37. **Repair damage**. Be socially sensitive to your emotional impact on others and mend the damage you create. You can think of this as cleaning up after yourself. And you can't just do it, you must *do it sincerely*. Insincerity will further degrade the damaged relationship, so you must recognize that you made a mistake before you apologize. Everyone knows human relationships sustain damage from time to time—that is the status quo and is acceptable. What is unacceptable is not repairing damage when it occurs.

38. **Accept sincere apologies**. Go ahead, forgive and forget. If you are offered a sincere apology, accept it. Everyone makes mistakes or mishandles pressure, and sometimes this leads to a socially destructive interaction. What matters is that the person has recognized it, realized he or she was at fault, and reached a hand out to you. Accept it, and do not extract anything more than you are offered. Exploiting a moment like this is worse than the original offense and should be clearly proscribed.

39. **Respect others' time and calendars**. If you are going to be late, show respect for others by letting them know. It is inconsiderate to let them find out you are late by waiting a long time. Also, respect others' calendars as well. Forcing others to rearrange their plans because you didn't plan adequately in advance is unacceptable.

40. **Show coworkers you see them as an equal**. Hold the door open for them, especially if they are carrying something; when they drop something, bend down and pick it up; press the Open Door button on the elevator if you hear or see someone approaching; if the elevator is crowded, step outside so others can get off; lastly, do not rudely push your way out of the elevator if it is crowded; rather, politely announce this is your floor so others can step aside.

You may read this list and think "This is obvious, trite, and nothing new." If all of this is in place, you are right. However, placing these guidelines into practice is new, and that is the opportunity—and doing so is free! Productive behavior is a real thing. I have never seen these mutually respectful practices broadly embraced at work. So, make doing so an imperative and reap a much larger return on human capital for no up-front investment—other than a little time. To me, behaving politely and productively is everyone's job.

Giving versus Getting

An unselfish orientation is absolutely critical to shared success. Here are some closing thoughts on what that means:

Think not how much you were helped but how much help you gave.

Think not about how much you composed but how much was composed because of you.

Think not about whether you are viewed as the best but if you performed your job to the best of your ability.

Think not about how you were treated but how you treated others.

Think not about whether you were treated with respect but whether you respected others.

Think not about whether you were hurt but whether you hurt others.

Think not about how many partners you have but to how many people you were a partner.

Think not about the sharpness of your tongue but the softness of your words, in case you have to eat them.

What is critical about these rules is that they help create warmth in relationships. Since a social system is a unique set of bonds, the quality and strength of these bonds is the substance that holds the fabric of the system together. The bonds can vary anywhere from closed to totally open, and the degree of openness determines whether it is easy or hard to collaborate, and whether it is meaningful. Once these bonds are open, however, the warmth that ensues drives the intensity of the collaboration.

This interaction is not all that different from the physical world. In the realm of chemical reactions, applying heat speeds chemical reactions. This is also true for social chemistry and social interactions. If the bonds go cold, productivity freezes or slows to a crawl. If warmth increases, however, business moves along more quickly. Thus, the world of physics applies to business productivity.

Citizenship Performance

The last item I will leave you with is another notion of behavior that is classified in academia as *citizenship performance*, which you can view as a variant of OCB since it too emphasizes the need for productive behavior. In a 2001 research paper titled "Personality Predictors of Citizenship Performance," Walter Borman, Louis Penner, Tammy Allen, and Stephan Motowidlo shared a great table summarizing their view of which behaviors really matter. Although the authors don't go into detail, their table is a good one, so I want to share it with you.[6]

Table 9.1   Revised Taxonomy of Citizenship Performance

A. Personal Support

Helping others by offering suggestions, teaching them useful knowledge or skills, directly performing some of their tasks, and providing emotional support for their personal problems. Cooperating with others by accepting suggestions, informing them of events they should know about, and putting team objectives ahead of personal interests. Showing consideration, courtesy, and tact in relations with others as well as motivating and showing confidence in them.

Subdimensions

Helping—Helping others by offering suggestions about their work, showing them how to accomplish difficult tasks, teaching them useful knowledge or skills, directly performing of their tasks, and providing emotional support for their personal problems.

Cooperating—Cooperating with others by accepting their suggestions, following their lead, and putting team objectives over own personal interests; informing others of events or requirements that are likely to affect them.

Table 9.1   Revised Taxonomy of Citizenship Performance

Courtesy—Showing consideration, courtesy, and tact in relations with others.

Motivating—Motivating others by applauding their achievements and successes, cheering them on in times of adversity, showing confidence in their ability to succeed, and helping them to overcome setbacks.

B. Organizational Support

Representing the organization favorably by defending and promoting it, as well as expressing satisfaction and showing loyalty by staying with the organization despite temporary hardships. Supporting the organization's mission and objectives, complying with organizational rules and procedures, and suggesting improvements.

Subdimensions

Representing—Representing the organization favorably to outsiders by defending it when others criticize it, promoting its achievements and positive attributes, and expressing own satisfaction with the organization.

Loyalty—Showing loyalty by staying with the organization despite temporary hardships, tolerating occasional difficulties and adversity cheerfully and without complaining, and publicly endorsing and supporting the organization's mission and objectives.

Compliance—Complying with organizational rules and procedures, encouraging others to comply with organizational rules and procedures, and suggesting procedural, administrative, or organizational improvements.

C. Conscientious Initiative

Persisting with extra effort despite difficult conditions. Taking the initiative to do all that is necessary to accomplish objectives even if not normally a part of own duties, and finding additional productive work to perform when own duties are completed. Developing own knowledge and skills by taking advantage of opportunities within the organization and outside the organization using own time and resources.

Subdimensions

Persistence—Persisting with extra effort to complete work tasks successfully despite difficult conditions and setbacks, accomplishing goals that are more difficult and challenging than normal, completing work on time despite unusually short deadlines, and performing at a level of excellence that is significantly beyond normal expectations.

Initiative—Taking the initiative to do all that is necessary to accomplish team or organizational objectives even if not typically a part of own duties, correcting non-standard conditions whenever encountered, and finding additional work to perform when own duties are completed.

Self-Development—Developing own knowledge and skills by taking courses on own time, volunteering for training and development opportunities offered within the organization, and trying to learn new knowledge and skills on the job from others or through new job assignments.

Source: Walter C. Borman et al., "Personality Predictors of Citizenship Performance," *International Journal of Selection and Assessment* 9, no. 1/2 (March/June 2001). Available at www.rc.usf.edu/~jdorio/ Personality/Personality%20predictors%20of%20citizenship%20performance.pdf.

What you see in the table and what I have suggested in this chapter are prosocial behaviors. These are highly productive behaviors, but the leaderships' behavioral impact has the greatest effect of all. An authentic and prosocial leader has an enormous positive impact across the organization. This behavior sets a highly productive tone, and it is powerful. So, in the next chapter, we delve into the importance of prosocial, servant leadership.

Notes

1. Dennis W. Organ, "The Motivational Basis of Organizational Citizenship Behavior," *Research in Organizational Behavior* 12 (1990): 47.
2. Dennis W. Organ, "Organizational Citizenship Behavior: It's Construct Clean-Up Time," *Human Performance* 10, no. 2 (1997): 86.
3. Ibid., p. 90. Walter C. Borman is a Doctor of Industrial/Organizational Psychology at the University of South Florida. He has written more than 300 journal articles, books, and book chapters concentrated in the areas of citizenship performance, personnel selection, performance measurement, and personality assessment. Stephan J. Motowidlo is a professor of Psychology at Rice University. He is broadly published in the area of Industrial/Organizational Psychology, with a PhD from the University of Minnesota.
4. Organ, "The Motivational Basis of Organizational Citizenship Behavior."
5. Ibid.
6. W. Borman et al., "Personality Predictors of Citizenship Performance," *International Journal of Selection and Assessment* 9, no. 1/2 (March/June 2001). Available at www.rc.usf.edu/~jdorio/Personality/Personality%20predictors%20of%20citizenship%20performance.pdf.

CHAPTER 10

The Servant Leader

Prosocial and Authentic

The leaders who work most effectively, it seems to me, never say "I." And that's not because they have trained themselves not to say "I." They don't think "I." They think "we"; they think "team." They understand their job to be to make the team function. They accept responsibility and don't sidestep it, but "we" gets the credit. . . . This is what creates trust, what enables you to get the task done.

—PETER F. DRUCKER

This chapter develops the notion of servant leadership, a paradigm in which the leader's needs are subservient to those of the workers. As in Chapter 4, I am going to use music as a metaphor to show how one conducts an information technology (IT) organization. With so many programming languages (our notes), technology shifts (musical eras), and tools (our instruments), IT has a much more complex orchestra from which its conductors must unlock great music. The hyperspecialization in IT ensures that the performers know their instruments far better than the conductor ever could, so focusing on creating an environment where they can give a great performance is paramount. In an IT organization of 1,000 people, 150 areas of knowledge specialization are not unusual, so the complexity is real and ever changing.

To craft an orchestra that flourishes, the conductor must remain outwardly focused, shaping the emotional, cognitive, and behavioral aspects of the group to unleash productive interactions and desirable outcomes. Encouraging prosocial behaviors, and modeling them yourself, increases the level of collaboration. It is the speed and quality of this interaction that drives productivity as the orchestra creates a group composition, co-creators, one and all. Like conducting, this form of leadership is an art, where style is best described using such words as *feeling*, *tempo* (pace of work), *insight*, and *observation*, with a "social recipe" and a unique blend of ingredients.

By peering inside this artistic expression of social intelligence, we see techniques that enhance one's ability to perform effectively and deliver a good performance. These techniques are guidelines you are free to embrace based on what feels comfortable and natural for you. Conducting group interaction, like a musical orchestra, is all about personal style. As no two individuals are alike, so no two conductors perform in an identical manner, yet both can be great. The social system one constructs, and the interaction style one employs, has as much to do with personal comfort as it does with effectiveness. You must be comfortable with yourself and your role in order to shape interaction around you. This comfort frees you to look outward to your external social environment, spawning social awareness, a sensitivity to the feelings and needs of those around you, and an ability to perceive the sentiment of the orchestra. It is out of this awareness that your conducting style will emerge—a public expression of how well you have grasped the emotional needs of the individuals performing for you, their social behavior, and how you can calibrate their interactions to create socioproductive outcomes.

Each great result in IT is the fusion of many individual minds and emotions that have become nearly one: a common vision, shared sentiment, collective excitement, and a chorus of voices sharing information and insight. Ultimately, you are a servant on a collective journey where the destination is a great performance, with every rehearsal leading to opening night. Here is a sense of just such an experience.

Opening Night

The sweat, fear, laughter, excitement, and anxiety point the way toward opening night. The conductor takes the pulse of the group's mood and warmly senses confidence and relaxation—the foundation of a giant success. It has been a difficult journey, beset by emotional ups and downs, but the resilience of the unit has been outstanding. The mutual support and trust have engendered an overcoming attitude, and obstacles that might have stopped the show have been easily overcome.

The conductor is very proud of the performers, carefully calibrating the tempo, refining the vision, providing guidance, and understanding the individual needs of each contributor and how they fit into the human social fabric. Their products are outstanding, and the creativity that has been unleashed is awe-inspiring. To design a high-performing, collaborative social system, the conductor has leveraged compatibilities, minimized destructive areas of social corrosion, reduced stress, and stimulated pockets of output. By tightly weaving this human fabric, gaps and disconnects in the product development cycle have been avoided. Indeed, it is true: *The quality of the outcome is merely a reflection of the social system that produced it.* In view of this fact, comfort levels are high and everything feels ready. It has been a truly cohesive effort, one where the conductor has successfully faded into the background. For the contributors, all that remains now is the quality of their first performance—their product showcase and launch.

In retrospect, even though there are many individual contributors, the development effort has been all about cohesion, bonds, rhythm, and group product creation; it is all about the people and their needs; it has been about creating a *social success* versus an individual one; it is all about everyone and no one. *The movement from selfish to selfless is complete.* A great performance beckons. The spotlight is theirs! The conductor is thrilled to remain in the background, relishing the contributors' joy and moment in the sun. Yes, the conductor truly is their servant.

Using Social Intelligence and Caring to Lead from Below

It is clear that the selfish, unfeeling leadership style that came to dominate the twentieth century has reached an evolutionary dead end. Trillions of dollars wasted on uncollaborative project failures clutter the 60-year chronicle that is IT. Collectively, these failures have produced an enormous desire for a silver bullet, but each breakthrough solution fails to end our cycle of disappointment. Worse yet, the high expectations and subsequent letdowns magnify our collective doubt and skepticism. All the while, our knowledge workers move in a trance from one effort to the next, wondering when someone will just rely on them and provide an environment in which they can flourish. For this leadership role, we have the servant conductor.

Leaders need to be authentic, trustworthy, empathetic, selfless, caring, upbeat (see Chapter 6), able to give work meaning, willing to speak with candor (openness), and relentlessly focused on maintaining open lines of communication. Ultimately, they must model prosocial behavior, knowing full well how contagious their behavior is. People don't do what you say; they do what you do. At an overarching level, leaders must be able to see the big picture, as this awareness enables them to communicate the importance of the work rather than just the need to get it done.

Servant conductors are sensitive to the needs of the social system, aware of each composer (if leading a team) and lower level conductors (if leading a department or division), their strengths and their weaknesses. These servant conductors see and understand the complete composition, sense how each portion of the work fits together, and can create harmony out of discord. Ultimately, they understand both the players and their performance styles, for *out of many they will fashion one*: a unified set of thoughts, people, actions, and shared objectives. Many minds emotionally wired together, forming an integrated nervous system that enables cooperative invention.

These servant conductors are also mindful of others' feelings and the need to provide each professional in the orchestra personal space. No matter how tempting, these conductors never emerge out of the orchestra pit to take someone else's instrument or baton in order to improve the harmony, even momentarily. These conductors know that embarrassing one of their performers will reduce their effectiveness because they have lost face. It is about the many, not the few. So the conductors attentively work to improve "the face" of every contributor, always sensitive to their needs and never embarrassing them in front of their fellow performers. By focusing on both individual and group needs, motivation levels rise and contributions increase.

In addition, the conductors provide both energy and imagination, emotionally sustaining the confidence of the orchestra. As each difficulty and disappointment is encountered, the leaders are resilient and jump into the fray to kick-start some possibility thinking (looking at alternative solutions) that relaxes the team; workable solutions become the focus instead of the impasse itself. This resilience is a critical attribute that sets the conductors apart from those who are insecure and uncertain, because they draw on an inner strength, confidence, and resolve, emboldening those around them, allowing the inevitable barriers to be surmounted time and time again. Problems are opportunities, and the confidence is infectious.

At all times they recognize the desires of the individuals but concentrate on protecting and meeting the needs of the group. Ultimately, success comes from the social system, not any single individual, least themself. They understand that group success springs from social systems fine-tuned for collaboration and mutual trust, where honesty and outflowing concern for one another predominate. This is a modern factory, a knowledge worker assembly system, animated by prosocial behavior, caring, empathy, trust, and concern for one another. These servant leaders realize its potential, see how important and different this human perspective is, and relish the opportunity to help their artists outperform. As it turns out, human understanding is a very powerful tool; as it also turns out, the collaborative social system is the means of production, and designing and tuning human-centric production is incredibly fulfilling.

Glimmers of just such a promising leadership style have emerged in the findings and observations of management experts, social scientists, and researchers. At first, disparate clues provided a weak outline of this emerging leader—compellingly different but not yet fully visible. Further research has filled in new pieces, giving the outline both shape and emotion: This leader is socially intelligent, sensitive to the needs of others, and focused on helping the social system succeed; this leader understands what it means to work in service of others; this leader is indeed the servant.

Conducting Styles

Nearly all men can stand adversity,
But if you want to test a man's character,
Give him power.

—UNKNOWN

It is clear that many leadership styles are successful. Although the level 5 leader (from Chapter 6 and also later in this chapter) is a servant, giving credit and empowering people, some highly successful businesspeople have been anything but that. Steve Jobs comes to mind immediately. Bright, driven, egotistical, arrogant, bearing down on people to diminish them, even untrustworthy at times, nevertheless he built the most valuable company in America; consequently, he is always cited as a great leader, highly admired around the world for what he was able to accomplish. He knew Apple's *why*, its mission, and therefore everything the company did challenged the status quo by relying on great engineering and design. Jobs was relentless in his pursuit of beautiful, intuitive products, and he got exactly what he wanted. Mark Zuckerberg also comes immediately to mind as someone who is introverted and not well liked—but he had a vision and relentlessly pursued it to bring Facebook to life. Neither of these people fits the profile of great leaders outlined in research and so many books on the topic. But they have been very successful at creating incredibly desirable products, which have spawned two great enterprises. I am going to provide my experience-based insights into a style that produces excellent results and is supported by the research; but the world is diverse, and so are the successful leadership styles. One size does *not* fit all.

The research does, however, shed light on one aspect of this paradox. Leaders are people others gladly follow. Not all of them are prosocial, but they do create trust. In Chapter 8, I reviewed the three types of trust as defined by Galford and Drapeau: organizational, strategic, and interpersonal. In the case of Steve Jobs, the last, interpersonal trust, would have been low, but the strategic trust would have been very high, so people gladly lined up behind him and put up with his quirks to reap the benefits of being in an organization with a brilliant strategy. Ultimately, people are motivated most by survival instincts, and Steve Jobs's ability to produce great wins, one after another, was the ultimate insurance policy. By working at Apple, you would not only survive, perhaps you would even flourish.

Servant Leadership in IT: Giving Credit While Silently Helping Drive Group Success

> It is a shame that so many leaders spend their time pondering their rights as leaders instead of their awesome responsibilities as leaders.
>
> —James C. Hunter

IT servant leaders work in the service of their organization, delivering great results for the company through the professionals. What they do is provide assistance, support, and caring, fight for the team, give to others, laugh with them, keep things light, reduce tension, and tend to group and individual needs. In this era of knowledge work, these servants are unselfish and socially intelligent conductors, whose function is to serve the needs of their people in order to boost productivity and output. Knowledge workers are quickly dominating the ranks of the workforce, and, more and more, they need to collaborate to accomplish their goals. In a positive departure with the past, those who *conduct* (lead) *from below* (servants) will achieve organizational speed and efficiency and be warmly embraced by troops who enthusiastically follow their lead. Employees in search of a ticket off Easter Island desire a productive and contented social environment, where *employer of choice* slogans aren't necessary.

By placing themselves in the position of servants, these leaders send a message that resonates with employees: These leaders are there to help them, not the leaders themselves. No part of the work, and no member of the team, is beneath them. Such leaders selflessly focus on helping the team succeed; they build trust and rapport, eliminating wasteful static, enabling producers to relax by weaving a cocoon within which they can create. The producers are the agenda and undivided focus; they are the only reason servant leaders are even needed.

> People do not care how much you know until they know how much you care.
>
> —John C. Maxwell

Servant leaders are grateful they are *leading* (not just observing) from below, and are focused on the staff's welfare. The orchestra is comforted by the conductor's leadership abilities and capacity to step in and shape the social system when distortions occur that jeopardize group success. As mutual trust and understanding evolve, the members of this social system recognize that personnel decisions are about their collective needs. They interpret individual departures as beneficial to the group because they too felt or recognized that,

that person was unable to harmonize with the other performers. Depersonalizing human decisions is vital: The strong contributors relax and produce once they observe that competence is both *seen and appreciated*. Within this social context, tough love is accepted and desired by those producing the value. The conductors always know, whatever they do, that *the entire orchestra is watching*.

As everyone connects actions to social benefits, lingering suspicions dissipate. The composers see fairness, respect, and meaningful decisions that communicate far louder than any words could—decisions grounded in an intimate understanding of group composition techniques and the ability to competently assess *human capital*. Now the good performers understand they will be seen, appreciated, and recognized for what they can contribute. This understanding satisfies their basic human need for recognition within the broader social group. An emotional calm seeps through every part of the social fabric.

Taken together, actions that focus on improving the collaborative social system imbue a sense of *fairness*, while accurate competence assessment imparts a sense of *honesty*. In this environment, solid producers feel *value protected* to the degree it is possible in a changing and competitive world. This feeling encourages the most productive composers to produce even more, an outcome that strengthens the social fabric, is highly desirable personally, and unleashes value for the corporation. Net-net, the social system accepts actions taken to safeguard its needs and integrity.

For the corporation, it is no longer about individual success but about social units, their cohesion, and their output. A productive social system materializes to replace one where workers looked inside themselves to find connections, where individual achievement was celebrated under a group banner, and where words failed to match deeds.

We now know that high performance requires togetherness. For this reason, the conductor applies an emotional substance to bind the social fabric together: *trust*. As social animals, this substance is a crucial ingredient in both our chemistry and the survival of our species, because humans are not the fastest, strongest, or fiercest of animals. In cohesion there was and is strength—strength enough to put humans in charge of our planet. Mutual trust led to unity, power, survival, and accomplishment. From a Darwinian perspective, one could say that the human success story is about the *social cohesion that emerged to emotionally connect us*.

Here actions speak louder than words; here a trusting social environment is fashioned from both honesty and truth; here the performers breathe easy. In this unspoiled atmosphere, the composers open up and begin to share their thoughts and feelings with one another. Slowly they are understood; and gradually their desires are heard. This transparency enables the conductor to glean critical insight for shaping the organization. The dialogue becomes constructive and more valuable as trust and mutual respect grow. Socially enabled learning ignites as trust strengthens the connections between group members and servant leadership reveals its potential. High-value output is on its way for the individuals, group, and corporation.

The counterproductivity of hidden agendas is understood to be a wasteful and destructive relic of the past. Selfish individuals, who formerly concealed their intentions, reform their behavior in order to survive within social units that rely on trust and openness rather than deceit—if not, the social immune system rises to neutralize their destructive tendencies. In this culture, the precious cycles formerly squandered unraveling hidden agendas across the organization are now put to productive use—productivity and the pace of work quicken. The positive reception for truthful and honest behavior brings issues and roadblocks into the daylight, where they are openly dealt with and eliminated. All see it is safe to speak here; all understand that success is a group activity, where servant leaders leave the bows to the performers.

In a musical performance, the conductor is seen vibrantly leading the orchestra from the podium. There the conductor stands, on display, guiding the orchestra while simultaneously delivering a performance of his or her own. The conductor energetically moves the baton and erupts with visible emotion as a crescendo is reached. During the program, the conductor may share the spotlight with celebrity musicians (e.g., first violin), graciously introducing them to the audience. Clearly, though, this is the conductor's orchestra, moment, accomplishment, and the glory is predominantly his or hers. The audience waits for the conductor's arrival; the elevated position on the podium and the forward bow that everyone sees send an unambiguous message: This is my orchestra, and I have brought you this outcome.

How different the collaborative and shared nature of IT is. The orchestra will underperform with this form of center-stage leadership. To deliver the greatest performance, the podium must be below, not above, the orchestra. The conductor must stand alone in the orchestra pit, the *servant leader*, gently guiding the flow, always visible to the musicians but often not to the audience. This arrangement produces the ultimate performance, memorable to both the orchestra and the audience, the one that creates the most beautiful music, inspiring to all, yet achieved using an invisible hand—a sensitive social baton, unseen by all but the performers.

In this situation, the performers get most of the credit, and they perform vigorously, knowing the spotlight is theirs. The show is all about them, the 100 seats in the orchestra, not the lone servant who leads them. Listen, look, and appreciate the beautiful music that each composer is creating for you in this emotionally cooperative work. The individual is important but never the focus. It is about the production of the many, not the few.

Jim Collins' *Harvard Business Review* article on level 5 leadership identified humility around others as a predictor of management success.[1] The most productive leaders of all are self-effacing, freely share credit, are biased toward meeting the needs of the people, and focus on their mission—the will to succeed. These management traits are just what the *composing orchestra* calls for.

Conducting in this manner requires deep trust, the highest level of personal security, and deep insight into each of the performers. When artfully done, it creates that elusive moment of truth where the audience clamors for an encore and wishes every composition could be just like this one.

But, alas, the source of this type of human social performance is not visible to most and is therefore not measured, reported, or valued; unfortunately, it is as subtle as it is beautiful. Regrettably, the socially intelligent actions that skillfully shape a great performance go unseen because of our learned insensitivity and social blindness. Performances of this quality happen when the conductor's art is practiced in silence, when it is felt and not seen. It is not boastful but considerate. Our existing selection processes pass these unsung heroes by, and they remain the exception rather than the rule.

So, for the servant leader to be appreciated, an informed audience that is perceptive enough to see and applaud an *invisible performance* is required. But today we don't even know we should look for such a performance. In fact, expectations demand a *visible* performance from the conductor—if we don't see the machines running, how could anything have been produced? Consequently, most leaders fall prey to the pressure and create a cult of personality that short-circuits the possibility of a memorable composer-centric performance. Output suffers. IT failure is always a failure of leadership.

Academic Views

An incredible amount of research on leadership has been produced; it is an age-old topic. As you go through the research, you discover that they frequently use the term *ethical leadership*. To me, ethics has a very specific meaning in corporate America. When you use the academic term, you have to immediately describe what is meant, because it refers to a broad set of management traits. Therefore, I much prefer to use *authentic and prosocial leadership*, especially given the number of leaders who are ethically challenged at this moment.

I have read many academic definitions of ethical leadership, yet the one by R. Edward Freeman and Lisa Stewart resonated. According to these authors, ethical leaders:

1. Articulate and embody the purpose and values of the organization.
2. Focus on organizational success rather than on personal ego.
3. Find the best people and develop them.

4. Create a living conversation about ethics, values, and the creation of value for stakeholders.
5. Create mechanisms of dissent.
6. Take a charitable understanding of others' values.
7. Make tough calls while being imaginative.
8. Know the limits of the values and ethical principles they live.
9. Frame actions in ethical terms.
10. Connect the basic value proposition to stakeholder support and societal legitimacy.[2]

Bill George is a professor of management practice at Harvard Business School but for over decade he was also chief executive officer of Medtronic, a world leader in medical technology. He has a great blog on which he offers very valuable perspectives that are worth poring over on your own. He has written extensively about *authentic leadership*, and lists five traits these leaders exhibit:

1. Pursuing their purpose with passion
2. Practicing solid values
3. Leading with their hearts as well as their heads
4. Establishing connected relationships
5. Demonstrating self-discipline[3]

In the same article, he goes on to say:

No individual achievement can equal the pleasure of leading a group of people to achieve a worthy goal. When you cross the finish line together, there's a deep satisfaction that it was your leadership that made the difference. There's simply nothing that can compare with that.

I enjoyed reading George's thoughts on leadership, because he understands how important it is to keep the needs of the people in mind. In an article titled "Why Leaders Lose Their Way," he characterizes leaders getting off track in terms that really resonated with me. He says:

By focusing on external gratification instead of inner satisfaction, leaders find it difficult to stay grounded. They begin to lose touch with reality, even if the ability to define reality accurately was a key quality that brought them success in the first place. Typically, these leaders reject the honest critic who holds up a mirror to them and "speaks the truth to power." Instead, they surround themselves with sycophants who tell them what they want to hear. Over time, these leaders lose the capacity for honest dialogue, as others learn not to confront them with reality or the truth.[4]

There are so many leadership books available, I will leave it to you to explore the topic on your own. Many cover the topic of servant leadership. You can be a servant leader yourself by being outwardly focused on the needs of others—the group—and by giving tough love when it is necessary. Being a leader in service of others is real and very valuable. I hope you embrace it.

Moving the Group from "I Get It" to "I See It"

One of the key things servant leaders at all levels need to do is to stimulate the sharing of discrete concepts and facts so they are collectively grasped by many minds. This is conceptual alignment across a large team—a moment of shared comprehension—and it is nothing short of a breakthrough created by individuals sharing thoughts and ideas openly, freely, unselfishly, worried about the team more than themselves. Some people grasp the concepts quickly, others less so. But a team that cares about one another will unselfishly invest the time needed to turn words and pictures into collective understanding; it is a conversion process that creates neural connections in different parts of the brain—each and every individual's. If this process fails, the misunderstandings turn into defects and gaps later on.

If the social system is highly collaborative, you achieve *conceptual unity*. The cliché is "getting everyone on the same page," but in a highly conceptual art like IT, the reality is closer to achieving a shared vision of the image hidden within a complex set of puzzle pieces. (Remember, you can never see, touch, or feel the solution beyond the outer edge—reports, user interface, etc.) Comprehension emerges as these pieces are connected together by each team member, until the full image emerges. Building these connections is an aptitude, with some people able to quickly see the big picture. This need is where a tuned-in conductor must provide insight and guidance to the full orchestra.

As the orchestra grows in size, many productivity cycles are wasted if shared understanding and direction are not firmly established. A large system is like a puzzle with many sections, each of which must be comprehended before the big picture emerges. The overall conductor provides the orchestra with the big picture, which shows how the subsections fit together, and the leaders of the subsections can then see where they fit in. If left to the group, individual needs and position within the social hierarchy will influence the shape of the framework, yielding distortion that must be later corrected.

Remember, composition and vision are two very different skills, and although many people have both, they rarely excel at both. The conductors must provide these skills themselves, or through a team member; otherwise, a vacuum will exist that gets filled slowly and, most likely, haphazardly. Also, the speed and accuracy of comprehension is a key productivity driver; the faster the vision is formed, the quicker the project moves—the quicker people move from "I get what we have to do" to "I see what I have to build, and can build it." If you can't see it, then you can't build it—you are just groping in the dark. The mind illuminates the objective, and for those who lack strong visualization skills, the picture is given to them through words.

With very little input, then, conductors and composers must be able to conceptualize their pieces and where they fit within the entire puzzle. Although hundreds of people may be working in teams that combine individual pieces into complete sections, the final product must begin with a clear outline. This is where the composer's and lead designer's visualization and abstraction skills come into play. By absorbing the high-level desires of the customer, an overall framework emerges that captures the multidimensional essence of the work—the border of the puzzle and the shape of the individual sections.

With a clear image visible, communication skills now come to the forefront, as the vision is shared using pictures and words to communicate a conceptual framework of what the composers have been asked to create. This outline defines the edges of the puzzle, establishing boundaries within which the composers will operate. When communicated clearly, a shared visual image of the final product exists across the entire orchestra, and conceptual unity has been achieved. Progress moves comfortably forward, within clear creative boundaries.

From this vision, the conductors' experience also allows them to establish gut sizing for both scope and complexity. Always socially sensitive to human capacities, conductors make sure the puzzle is not grander in scope than their orchestra is capable of grasping. As discussed in Chapter 6, the mind has a physical limitation called working memory—the number of items that the conscious mind can manage at any one time.

If you violate the working memory capacity of people by making a project too large (i.e., too many interrelated pieces that need to be considered at once), work slows as they struggle to connect the myriad dots. It is a visual process. If you can't visualize the many interconnections, trouble emerges, and people find that gaps have developed. So, the project becomes slow moving and highly unproductive.

In addition, interpersonal communication increases as the number of touch points between different areas of the social system expands to mirror the complexity of the puzzle. Each group of composers finds it needs to involve an expanding group of people as the hidden scope becomes visible.

Slowly but surely, the team members try to absorb all of the interconnections between the pieces, but because the scope is too large, some pieces are put aside (out of "sight," out of mind), some pieces are developed in great detail (I see that and am comfortable), and some connections between components remain mentally out of scope. People are simply overwhelmed. This happens across the initiative, yielding poorly thought-out pieces, disconnects, gaps, rework, slowness, and open items galore. The project begins to drag on as open items accumulate, and scope and cost ratchet upward. This is the bane of a mega-initiative that attempts to boil the ocean.

If you think a project is too big at the start, just wait until the many layers underneath are exposed as comprehensive understanding dawns.

But, alas, total awareness and resignation always arrive too late. Large trophy systems require significant up-front selling and executive buy-in. Large commitments are made, and reputations are on the line. The sad truth is masked by misplaced optimism until the true cost and scope are undeniable. It is then that survival takes over as the pain overwhelms even the most strident supporters. The true state of affairs is dealt with, and the effort is written off or a small deliverable is pumped up as a means of declaring victory. The legacy of this decision is difficult to wipe away.

In complex group endeavors, leaders have to tune in to others, making sure their own feelings are never the focus, but rather the feelings and mood of the team. To accomplish this, servant leaders carefully manage their own emotions and help improve the sentiment of those whom they serve. They are socially intelligent and outwardly focused at all times. As we see in Chapter 11, this outward focus is pivotal and is what sets the great IT leader apart.

Notes

1. Jim Collins, "Level 5 Leadership: The Triumph of Humility and Fierce Resolve," *Harvard Business Review* (January 2001): 70. Available at http://hbr.org/2005/07/level-5-leadership-the-triumph-of-humility-and-fierce-resolve/ar/1.
2. R. Edward Freeman and Lisa Stewart, "Developing Ethical Leadership," Business Roundtable Institute for Corporate Ethics, 2006. Available at www.corporate-ethics.org/pdf/ethical_leadership.pdf.
3. Bill George, "Truly Authentic Leadership," October 30, 2006. Available at www.billgeorge.org/page/truly-authentic-leadership.
4. Bill George, "Why Leaders Lose Their Way," 2011. Available at www.billgeorge.org/page/why-leaders-lose-their-way.

CHAPTER 11

Social and Emotional Intelligence

The Organizational Canvas Meets the Social Paintbrush

Life would be stunted and narrow if we could feel no significance in the world around us beyond that which can be weighed and measured with the tools of the physicist or described by the metrical symbols of the mathematician.

—SIR ARTHUR EDDINGTON

Much has been written about social and emotional intelligence in the past 30 years. I first came across this subject through Howard Gardner, who wrote about intrapersonal and interpersonal intelligences in his 1983 book *Frames of Mind*. Intrapersonal intelligence is an understanding of self, "an access to one's own feeling life—one's range of affects or emotions: the capacity instantly to effect discriminations among these feelings and, eventually, to label them, to enmesh them as a means of understanding and guiding one's behavior."[1] The second, interpersonal intelligence, is focused on others, and this is what is also commonly referred to as social intelligence. It provides "the ability to notice and make distinctions among other individuals and, in particular, among their moods, temperaments, motivations, and intentions." Gardner goes on to say that "in an advanced form, interpersonal knowledge permits a skilled adult to read the intentions and desires—even when these have been hidden—of many other individuals and, potentially, to act upon this knowledge—for example, by influencing a group of disparate individuals to behave along desired lines." What Gardner has in fact done is lay out a basic model for what has since become known as emotional intelligence.

Daniel Goleman brought this subject into mainstream discourse. His 1996 book, *Emotional Intelligence*, included references to Gardner's work, but where Gardner had a single chapter devoted to this subject area, Goleman dug deep. If you haven't read it, I highly recommend you do, as emotional intelligence, more than IQ, determines people's level of success in business. Building a greater degree of awareness will help you, and the book is an eye-opener, given its breadth of content and the fascinating real-life accounts woven throughout the narrative. Goleman later went on to become a founding member of the Consortium for Research on Emotional Intelligence in Organizations, which is a great information resource.[2] Its mission "is to advance research and practice of emotional and social intelligence in organizations." You should review this as well, as the consortium has done a great job of highlighting the importance of EQ at work.

You can download the Emotional Competency Framework, which looks at both the intra- and interpersonal (social) aspects of emotional intelligence.[3] It breaks both of these down into an ability to understand and use your own emotions while also understanding emotions in others. It is essentially the same framework that Gardner used, but the consortium does a much better job of defining it, and breaks emotional intelligence down into personal competence and social competence.

Personal and Social Competence

> What is necessary to change a person is to change his awareness of himself.
>
> —ABRAHAM MASLOW

Emotional intelligence is vital to success, and research has shown it is a determining factor in your advancement. In fact, "[emotional intelligence] accounts for 15% to 45% of your success on the job. (Your IQ, by comparison, is said to account for less than 6%)."[4] To start, consider personal competence, which is your source of self-awareness, enabling you to intimately understand your own feelings, act with self-confidence, and know what you are good at so that you don't overstep your capabilities; personal competence also enables self-regulation, which gives you control over impulses and key behaviors, such as trustworthiness, conscientiousness, and adaptability; last, it can provide self-motivation so that you desire advancement, have the drive to achieve it, and have an ability to stay optimistically committed to group/organizational goals.

To me, the social competence perspective gets to the heart of collaboration in information technology (IT). These competencies are vital to success, because building solutions is about group, not individual, success, as I've pointed out many times. Nothing matters more. I believe the concept of social intelligence is critically important, yet we do not have a single word to describe it in the English language. It is a crucial skill for creating harmony and unity. It is also a key governor of whether group tasks will translate into results.

Let's take a look at how the consortium breaks out this area of EQ. At a high level, social competence has two major dimensions: social awareness and the social skill to work effectively with others. The social awareness consists of empathy, which I have covered in considerable depth; it also has a service orientation, which is a sensitivity to others' needs and a desire to serve them (IT is at its essence a service business). People with this competence have an ability to develop others (certainly critical given the rate of change and the shortage of leaders and successors) and to work effectively with a diverse group of people (IT is probably the most diverse profession, with people from everywhere). Last, they have political awareness so that they can see the power structure and read the political tea leaves (IT is organizationally very complex, as it is an enterprise function).

The social skills include:

- Influence, which is the ability to persuade people by presenting information cogently (helping the business to see the potential of new technologies or employees to grasp why something is important and therefore laden with meaning).
- Communication, which is being able to listen well and communicate clearly (and, in IT, translating from technical to business with ease).
- Leadership, which is developing enthusiasm across the group while bringing everyone onto the same page (an enormously important part of the job).
- Driving change, which is what IT does with every project and the ability to gain acceptance for it by being a champion.
- Collaboration and cooperation, which were discussed at length in Chapter 8.
- Building bonds, another skill that is ever so vital to pulling the social fabric of IT together.
- Conflict management, which is self-evident and vital because the fact that there are so many solutions to any problem in IT means that preventing conflict and protecting relationships is a core need.
- Team capabilities, such as sharing credit and helping one another, further strengthening bonds and connections.

The fact we do not have a single word to describe this critical form of intelligence is a gap that needs to be remedied. I suggest we give birth to a new word: *sogence*.

sogence (social intelligence). n. Sensitivity and awareness to the needs and feelings of others, whether individuals or groups; an ability to take others into account in your interactions, statements, expressions, behavior, and deeds; the ability to shape group social interaction with the express intent of creating harmony, respect, collaboration, and mutual trust.

sogent adj. To possess or display sogence, as in a sogent leader, a sogent decision, or a sogent act.

Sogence in Action

Sogence is a critical skill, an indispensable driver of success. Every good IT leader must grow it, or the corporation will witness underperformance of its IT investments and noticeable shortcomings in its business solutions and infrastructure. Consequently, management will become unhappy, and the desire for change will grow, until they engage "external experts." These outside experts add a disharmonic dimension to the social milieu, levering up the complexity, risk, and cost of whatever is being done. The ramifications are often far reaching.

> If you can learn a simple trick, Scout, you'll get along a lot better with all kinds of folks. You never really understand a person until you consider things from his point of view, until you climb inside of his skin and walk around in it.
>
> —ATTICUS FINCH IN *To Kill a Mockingbird* (1962)

Sogent leaders are emotionally intelligent, deeply in touch with themselves while also deeply feeling others' needs, desires, and fears. Their perceptual ability provides an intense awareness of the internal and external (business partners) social environments. Because of their deep and meaningful understanding of the collective interactions that go on around them, they sense how to guide and shape productive social collaboration. This soft skill—unquantifiable and closer to art than science—enables them to turn the smooth operation of the orchestra into a craft. Such a distinctly communal orientation is part of our endowment as a social species, our heritage, and one of our basic intelligences. Like other intelligences, it occurs in degrees, with the gifted capable of sogent leadership.

As Yogi Berra said, "You can observe a lot just by watching." So, sogent leaders observe intently, employing all of their senses to connect emotionally with the social fabric. Leveraging socially intelligent insights, they operate in the emotional service of their orchestra members. Sogence is a baton they use to set the mood and tempo of the entire orchestra—they are the corporate conductors, lifting everyone's mood and feeling until flow, productivity, and striking results are unlocked. They are always *selfishly unselfish*, focused on the needs of others, facilitating collective goals and group success. The selfishness is symbiotic, in that it serves the needs of the conductors, orchestra, and corporation in an intensely human-focused manner.

For sogent conductors, *people are the instruments*. These conductors perform skillfully, honing their social insight to bring meaning to as many individuals as possible. By doing so, they unlock the creative potential of the orchestra, help it achieve a state of flow, and deliver a brilliant performance; they want members to feel good, to connect with one another, so as to tightly weave the human fabric that forms the communication backbone. When interacting with individual members of the team, these conductors are outwardly focused: looking, observing, feeling, learning—taking in the behavioral landscape that surrounds them. This heightened understanding leads to *considerate decisions* that are warmly embraced by the composers (programmers) who recognize that *the agenda is in their best interests*. The payoff for companies like Apple and Google that choose to rely on and energize their own workers is market leadership—so long as the business strategy is a sound one. You cannot spin gold from salt water, no matter how warmly interconnected everyone is.

To create the optimal milieu, conductors must be sensitive to how each member is performing. One must be able to spot subtle changes in demeanor, such as a facial expression that hides sadness or worry; a raised tone of voice that alerts you to rising emotional temperature; or the distance between two individuals who normally sit together and unexpectedly are not. Pay attention to see subtle changes, then evaluate their importance versus the backdrop of individuals, their roles, and the health of the projects they are on. Once you decide what to do, intervene if doing so has productive value.

Remember, emotional state changes are clues that invite you to gently probe or investigate the source. Clearly, people have bad days, and every sentiment change isn't meaningful—although noticing and responding drives up productivity, regardless of the root cause. If you miss or ignore important signals, the quality of the performance will slowly deteriorate and productivity will begin to slip. Like corrosion, each disconnect starts small, expands outward, and then becomes conspicuous. At its onset, social corrosion is easy to ignore because it appears inconsequential—but this is just a comfortable illusion. If you ignore the situation and have to get involved later, it won't be at a time or manner of your choosing. The damage will be directly proportional to the importance of the affected bonds and how much time has passed. Keep in mind that with each passing day, damage accumulates because broken bonds prevent information that needs to be exchanged from being exchanged. It's just that simple.

To maintain working connections across the orchestra, the door (or cubicle) of an outwardly focused leader or coworker is always open, and performers wrestling with interpersonal issues understand that others are there to listen and help, not judge them. When coworkers show sincere interest in each other's challenges, an element of calmness is felt across the group because each producer has strong emotional support to fall back on. Individuals facing challenges welcome an opportunity to speak openly and honestly about their concerns. They find the dialogue itself comforting, and are happy to share what they feel they should do and are receptive to others' suggestions. Openly caring people don't judge; they just help wherever and however they can. Doing this keeps connections open and information flows unimpeded.

By bringing understanding and insight into individual and group moods, socially intelligent teams toil to elevate everyone's sense of well-being. Freeing the human spirit to create, relax, and perform is the necessary precondition to great achievement. This isn't to say that toxic environments produce nothing; they just don't produce greatness. Dispirited workers still have self-esteem, so they soldier on. But in a human-dependent art like IT, where solving puzzles and unraveling solutions is the chief objective, a dearth of positive energy and connectedness means progress is slow to nonexistent; mediocrity abounds, and everyone wonders why people aren't doing their jobs well.

For people with high degrees of sogence, work is their laboratory, and they are always striving to improve the social chemistry. They enhance their social insights through observation and experience and use a variety of tools to peer more deeply. Let's see what avenues are available.

Understanding Expression: A Social Skill from Our Past

The most important thing in communication is hearing what isn't said.

—PETER F. DRUCKER

Socially sensitive conductors stay aware of nuances in body language and notice changes in this outward manifestation of inner feelings. Being highly perceptive and socially aware, they absorb the information being fed to them through nonverbal clues in their surroundings. This tool is both art and science that business has mostly ignored, yet it is the sole subject of a number of books. If you want to know more, seek them out and read them.

One of interest is *What Every Body Is Saying*, written by Joe Navarro, an ex-FBI agent who spent his career reading deceptive behaviors and body language.[5] You won't become proficient at reading body language just by reading books; like everything else, it involves practice to internalize the knowledge so you can read the signals.

Interestingly, Charles Darwin spent a lifetime keenly observing his surroundings. He was externally focused on the world around him, even though he was an introvert. His treatise on the subject, *The Expression of the Emotions in Man and Animals*, was first published in 1871 and posited the notion that human emotions are universal in nature, crossing cultural and national boundaries. To prove this was true, he asked explorers and travelers to record whether the non-Europeans they encountered used specific emotional expressions in a variety of circumstances. From the answers he received back, he concluded: "It follows . . . that the same state of mind is expressed throughout the world with remarkable uniformity; and this fact is in itself interesting, as evidence of the close similarity in bodily structure and mental disposition of all the races of mankind."[6] Darwin was way ahead of his time, and neurological studies have proven the bulk of his theories correct. Paul Ekman, a noted psychologist and author on emotion, released an updated version of Darwin's book, the third edition, in 1998, with introductory comments highlighting the unparalleled depth of Darwin's original work.[7]

This book does a remarkable job cataloging the wide range of expressions, with examples, pictures, and insightful explanations. Since he was interested in proving that man and animals shared common evolutionary roots, he covers both in the book. Although this book was ignored for over 90 years, it is more relevant than ever. If your reading list is already long, you can save time by focusing on just the human emotions, which are covered separately.

Everyone responsible for leading knowledge workers should expand their understanding of expressions. Sensitivity to the emotional well-being of others is critically important as plans and commitments are made, teams are formed, people explain options and decisions, and you guide and shape the emotional state of the team or orchestra. Given the universal nature of this human response, each expression is a potential source of valuable data when managing global teams, where language and culture are barriers. This information represents raw, unmanipulated input that guides you to the truth—the operational state of mood, interaction, and relationships. The subtext to every conversation and interaction, it is both a beacon and a guide.

Although I cannot prove that emotional expression guided interaction among our early human ancestors prior to the emergence of the language, it is the case today among primates and social animals, such as dogs. In all likelihood, emotional expression was our first form of communication, the window into our emotions. It guided interactions then and now, although this facility is not taught in schools and not embraced as the valuable tool it most certainly is.

The emotional brain (limbic system) evolved first, followed by the cerebral cortex. From this emotional foundation, higher human capabilities (e.g., cognitive thinking, speech, reasoning, etc.) literally evolved on top of it. As a civilization, we have become focused on cognitive, IQ-based skills and have disregarded the emotional ones that support our gut instincts.

We encounter expressions every day of our lives, and the clichés "poker face" and "open book" reflect our innate understanding that the face really does communicate emotion. Although clichés have evolved to describe non-verbal forms of communication, they are not formally recognized as a tool. Why not? The human face is a lens through which we can peer into the inner emotional states of those on whom we rely.

All leaders should be sensitive to the emotions of their people. Each movement, facial expression, and glance is the subtext of interactions taking place around you. These are the notes that need to be heard and adjusted when they are out of key; these are a cross-cultural means of communicating; and they are difficult to manipulate since many are involuntary (except for powerful actors), forming a language of their own. Honing this skill is a worthwhile investment since more communication is nonverbal than verbal, although the percentages are debated (some say 90 percent although I cannot find definitive proof for any percentage).

Good Vibrations: The Right Social Sentiment Energizes a Performance

What are some of the things you can do to increase the performance of your organization or team members? Anyone can improve their capability in this area just by observing, and making note of these observations to grasp what they mean. Clearly, mood and sentiment are enormous drivers of output, and unselfishness is a highly productive force. You can act on social insights to regulate the feelings and moods of your people. Because mood is contagious, it can spread one on one or downward like a current over the social network. Each of the next rules will help you grasp the threads of mind and emotion that constitute your team and weave them together using socially sensitive actions.

> **Rule #1: Sing people's praises by seeing the best in them**. Be observant. Everyone has a tapestry of skills, some less visible than others. It is very easy to see people's faults and weaknesses and criticize them to create a personal advantage by bringing them down. It is far more difficult to see the good, build people up, and guide them to reduce their weaknesses so that their strengths shine brighter. For that reason, instead of reinforcing negative perceptions by highlighting errors, highlight the quality of their compositions, so that their contribution is understood and seen by others the way you see it. Jointly relish the fact that they

are positioned correctly in the organization and the company is benefiting from their unique talent. If you are a coworker, you should build up your teammates, as the collective strength is what counts, not you as an individual. Patch the tapestry if you find holes, weave in new threads to add color and vibrancy, and draw the threads tight around you if they are becoming loose.

Rule #2: Energize the orchestra. Transmit the energy and excitement you feel to the team to liven them up. Mood is contagious, and nothing improves the energy and warmth of a team more than passing on a positive vibe. Optimism is contagious, and as it spreads, it energizes the orchestra.

Transmit confidence to help people overcome self-doubt when you see it or to counter doubt when it flows as an undercurrent. I have observed these undercurrents many times. Keep in mind that our survival instincts keep team members tuned in, and the need to uncover danger causes bad news (danger) to travel fast, even if it is incorrect. Dial into the group's mood. If you see it slipping, wander around, talk to everyone, and find out what is happening. Remember, if confidence wanes, protective behavior takes over, as people distance themselves from risk, especially those who are struggling the most, because helping them entwines you in their issue. Therein lies danger.

I once dedicated a town hall meeting to generate confidence by communicating why I was feeling so good about the team's performance, citing specific examples of progress that counteracted the negative, false news that was spreading. I won. People trusted me, they left the meeting energized, progress was greatly multiplied, and we delivered on our commitments. Mood and confidence are easily shattered. *It is upon shared trust that we build an energetic environment and group success.*

Rule #3: Repair the social fabric. Teams of ordinary people accomplish great things when the social fabric is strong and the chemistry supportive. Having led many turnarounds of failed and failing initiatives, I understand that there are always a few artists who need to be replaced. That said, if you transform the social system instead of replacing the people in it, you can move an orchestra from total failure to incredible accomplishment. The only explanation for this immense difference in performance is that the social system can be either a means of production or an impediment to it.

To recover from a failure, do the traditional process assessment, but focus as much, or more, on repairing the social fabric. As the conductor, you must create trust, repair frayed and broken social connections, build rapport with the key influencers (beacons within the network), assume full responsibility for success and failure (thus relaxing fearful minds), create laughter to displace tension, and generate applause that all can hear.

Rule #4: Be the best audience possible. Enjoy every victory, and be compassionate about every failure. Always let your excitement and passion be visible for all to see, and give both public and private applause for real accomplishments. Laugh along with others, and work to cheer up those who are down by helping them see the positives in what they have done and the potential in what they are doing. You are the audience, guiding emotion from below, so that your orchestra puts on the best performance possible. Cheer for them when it is deserved and sincerely enjoy what they are doing for the organization.

Rule #5: Use tough love where needed. Feedback is a form of caring. Make the time to talk with your workers, help them, and guide them, even when the message is not praise based. Do it because the feedback is needed. It is your job to contain destructive behavior, and the members of the orchestra are depending on you to tactfully deliver needed messages.

Rule #6: Think realistically; behave optimistically. The orchestra members understand what is possible and become anxious over goals they know are unachievable. The consequent fear of failure impairs the human infrastructure, as anxiety slows cognitive function, siphoning productive capacity toward unproductive thought. Honestly, the composers understand whether the objectives you have set are realistic, so be realistic at all times and be open to feedback when you are wrong. It's okay to set a difficult objective, but ask for the impossible, and your credibility will be diminished and your trustworthiness reduced. Said another way, support reality, and reality will be delivered; support the imaginary, and vapor will appear. Knowing the difference between the two is an experiential art.

Rest assured, however, that in spite of realistic objectives, difficulties will appear. Confront these adverse situations head-on, and be straight with the team. At all times, in spite of the adversity, be optimistic. As long as what you are asking for is possible, use optimism as a fuel to energize the team. The positive energy is contagious and spreads across the group like good news—but only if the optimism is sincere and fact based. Celebrate the small steps forward, and the big strides will follow.

Rule #7: Maximize tempo through social understanding. The orchestra creates with both tempo and mood. Providing both of these is the conductor's responsibility. The tempo, or pace, comes from the conductor's power to throttle activity levels up and down by starting projects, delegating additional work, and setting deadlines. If you know and understand your performers, you can play at a fast tempo, and the artists can keep up—but knowing your composers requires careful and ongoing observation. Vary the tempo so you can feel what pace is effective. Maximize the pace once you discover what it is.

Rule #8: Confront disharmony. Intervene to turn disharmony into harmony whenever you can. Try sensing the moods, human challenges, and difficulties facing the orchestra. Understanding, in this case, comes from experience—learning how to play an instrument through trial and error in the same way a batter takes thousands of swings or learning to conduct by leading many orchestras from small to large. Practice makes perfect. Start with simple observations and grow from there as you piece the larger picture together. It will happen—it just takes time and patience.

Rule #9: Build others' confidence. If other people can do it, you can, too. The conductor must work to remove the self-doubt that always creeps in—at the individual and, if infectious enough, at the team or division level. Confidence is critical, as each composer must solve problems he or she has never solved before. Often composers are using instruments for the first time, fearlessly climbing a steep learning curve. Be there to steady them, and catch them if they fall.

Rule #10: Unlock the team's motivation. Knowledge workers need to be energized to move into action and overcome the inertia that plagues projects early on. You should be sensitive to this and try to understand if any of the inertia is emotional in nature. It probably is. If you are truly tuned in to the orchestra and your coworkers, you can unblock the emotions and help work flow smoothly and evenly. The intense energy that is required to put a human social system in motion will give way to intrinsically generated momentum, as understanding grows, as fear of failure subsides, and as human factors like meaning create emotional energy, attachment, and drive. Help the process along however you can.

Rule #11: Create a resilient team. We build an energetic environment upon shared trust. Everyone stumbles. Applauding when someone gets up builds resilience. Getting knocked down is nothing; getting back up is everything. Reach out your hand and help people back onto their feet. Laugh it off with them. Knowing it is okay to stumble provides the reassurance needed to traverse rough ground.

Rule #12: Encourage respectful debate. As mentioned elsewhere in this book, harmony without debate is apathy. When you know someone has great ideas but is shy about sharing them, draw the person out. He or she needs to shine, so help and thank these people for contributing. If their contributions add to the debate, that's good, as long as it remains respectful. Introverted people are easy to defeat in a debate, because they withdraw. Help them, and reap the rewards of their insights.

Rule #13: Remove roadblocks. Tune in. You can quickly tell when someone is unwilling to share a resource or let go of an idea in the face of solid evidence to the contrary. Some professionals emotionally need to be right or always win. This is both frustrating and highly destructive, as individuals with this attitude quickly become bottlenecks. If they cannot overcome their own needs, step in and make sure the right thing gets done. This is a good coaching opportunity as well.

Rule #14: Help people find meaning in the work. You need to constantly tune in to the human quest for meaning and help your composers understand the importance of what they are doing. I have used meaning to create great motivation and actually have seen a well-targeted conversation noticeably change the level of drive right before my eyes. Spend time thinking about this.

Case in point: As I was writing this, the 2012 Summer Olympics had recently ended, and I couldn't help but notice how the team of the country hosting the Olympics improves remarkably every time. In fact, going back to 1956, the host team has achieved, on average, a 32 percent increase in total medals versus the Olympics just four years prior. Britain's performance showed a 38 percent increase this time. It is absolutely clear that the home court always confers advantage in athletic competition, but in the Olympics, the power of meaning created for the host stands out because the higher level of achievement is always visible.

For host athletes, the national limelight shines brightly; each of them has a chance to win the esteem of their nation since national pride is at stake. Here you see a few different drivers of meaning: patriotism, high self-esteem, and recognition—all of which play a part for every athlete, but they are magnified for the host country. The statistics prove this out. Meaning matters a lot.

Rule #15: Leave time each day for reflection. Schedule this on your calendar if you have to, and shut your door. You must observe, think, and reflect—not only about yourself and how well you are performing but about your people. If you have to do this on your commute, so be it. Many insights will crystallize, and you will become conscious of them if you just set aside time for these ideas to flow. Reflection is important and allows you to be mentally organized and digest the information that you have tuned in to.

Rule #16: Wander around. Get up, walk over to your coworkers, peers, and subordinates, and talk to them. E-mail slows down interaction and provides a feeling of progress when often it is actually retarding it. E-mail is missing all of the social cues gained through interaction, and this information represents a lot of the communication. Don't over-rely on e-mail and other forms of messaging. Everyone will adjust to your style.

Rule #17: Remember to smile, smile, smile. A smile is equivalent to an open door. It says you are approachable and upbeat and is an invitation to "come in." When you smile, you are sharing something positive, giving part of yourself to others. You are quietly communicating that you are happy with the present and that you like those around you. You are one with the social system. You gather so much more social input when it is clear you welcome it.

Rule #18: Remember, problems represent progress. The greatest thing about knowledge work is that you get paid to solve problems and create something that never existed before. People do the same thing for pleasure when they work on a crossword puzzle or other challenge. Go ahead, let go, enjoy the problems, and relish every challenge and solution. The social environment relaxes when problems are a welcome challenge and people know you understand the complexity. What a great business.

Rule #19: Seriousness is a veil—don't wear it. Walking around with a serious expression, even a stern one, sends a strong message: "I am unapproachable." It functions as a public veil that isolates you from the orchestra. Look too serious, and you cut off spontaneous communication with your composers and isolate yourself from the only source of real information available. If your nature is always serious, then lighten up to open two-way communication, which enhances productivity.

Rule #20: Be direct and concise. Remember, it is about them, not you. Everyone wants to know "we" are in this together; that we are not blame oriented; that saying what you think in a direct, polite, and concise way is welcome. Always look at the social implications of what you do and leverage every opportunity to build strong connections; maintain sensitivity to the social system around you and keep the industrial blinders off—this equipment is human.

If you follow these rules consistently, you will shape a very powerful social environment. The human equipment is not only socially intelligent, it is also highly creative, given the right environment and meaningful work. What corporations need now, more than ever, is innovation. We have treated our workers as parts and destroyed the social fabric not only of collaboration but of creativity. Now let's take a look at what you should do to flip the innovation switch back on.

Notes

1. Howard Gardner, *Frames of Mind* (New York: Basic Books, 1993), 237–243.
2. Consortium for Research on Emotional Intelligence in Organizations. Available at www .eiconsortium.org/index.html.
3. Ibid.
4. "Hiring Emotionally Smart" (*Harvard Management Update, 2000)*. Article reprint number U0009C, p. 3.
5. Joe Navarro, *What Every Body Is Saying* (New York: Harper Collins, 2008).
6. Charles Darwin, *The Expression of the Emotions in Man and Animals* (New York: Oxford University Press, 1998), 24.
7. Paul Ekman is a world-renowned PhD, professor, researcher, and prolific author who has studied emotion and facial expressions in a career spanning more than 50 years. He is now retired, and runs Paul Ekman Group, LLC, a small company that makes training and promotes new areas of research. More information available at www.paulekman.com.

CHAPTER 12

Designing an Innovative Culture

Imagination is more important than knowledge. Knowledge is limited. Imagination encircles the world.

—ALBERT EINSTEIN

I have stressed how important culture is to productivity. But ultimately, innovation is the enduring source of competitive advantage. Innovation is an outcome, a by-product of the culture you build, which, as I have stressed, is a result of thoughtful design.

Therefore, culture is the crucible in which the social chemistry of your organization crystallizes into a positive and supportive environment or one that is negative and poorly suited for creative work. It is the social environment that drives mood, sentiment, and desire and, if designed right, unlocks innovation. People can devote their emotional energy to productive (creating) or unproductive (worrying) activity. It is your call.

The innovation recipe is simple to describe. Build a bright, energetic, and creative team, develop a supportive culture, and grow deep institutional experience so there is abundant knowledge to drive creative innovation. On the surface it sounds simple, but the transformation takes time to complete, so stick with it, knowing patience is rewarded.

To transform your organization's innovation quotient (the other IQ), I am going to review the steps you can take to foster the creativity you desire. Although I recommend a series of steps, they aren't set in stone, and should be addressed based on situational needs. Also, these activities should proceed in parallel. Don't approach each one as a discrete project. They are all intertwined, and you will advance the fastest by making consistent progress in every area. At the end of the year, you will have had a meaningful impact. Your transformation will be well under way, although it will take longer to fully blossom.

Talent and Mood

Begin with talent. Every company has a talent acquisition process, so influence it to blend creative people into your department. Finding them will take good interviewing technique, because you aren't looking for just creative thoughts but creative outcomes. Some people are very creative but can't work well in teams and turn off people around them because of socially corrosive behaviors. Who needs great pearls if they remain trapped in oysters? Getting to the true track record and not blindly accepting the talk record is paramount. Obviously, back channels to people who have worked with the individual in the past are invaluable. Use them. That said, if you have a large organization, you already have plenty of creative talent.

Next, work on the mood. Organizations with a dark sentiment are emotionally closed, low-energy affairs that suppress creative drive and end up focused on safety instead. Upbeat, positive environments create zest, motivation, and desire, tapping people's potential energy rather than suppressing it. Remember, energy levels are elastic and can be pulled up or down. Push them up, and reap the high-performing benefits. Let the positive feelings flow through your social network, driving high-return interactions, where ideas are stimulated through open and honest conversation and creative juices flow freely.

Next, communicate and explain the importance of the work. Everyone wants to make an important contribution, and for knowledge workers, contributions come through meaning. If you can, speak to people individually, even in the hallway. Explain how their jobs relate to the greater goals of the enterprise and how important their assignment is. Doing this can tap the well of emotional energy that drives higher performance and unleashes creative flashes. Greater meaning becomes drive, and with enough emotional energy, the creative sparks will fire off.

The social environment really matters because safety-seeking behaviors are counterproductive. Such behaviors are found in organizations where antisocial behavior is allowed to create fear and stress. There are significant negative impacts on cognitive processes when an individual's security or esteem are threatened, as the limbic system (emotion) is stimulated to release neurotransmitters that stimulate the fight-or-flight reaction, essentially cutting off higher-level thought. If the stress is persistent, such as repetitive threats from a toxic leader, the neurotransmitters stay in the blood, causing stressed-out symptoms to emerge, including difficulty concentrating, watching out for negatives instead of focusing on work tasks, and anxious or racing thoughts. Professionals who are preoccupied like this are not going to innovate anything. Given the fact that information technology (IT) is at its root a creative endeavor, individuals who grind through each workday will not be productive. Was a great invention ever conceived by a person fleeing from a threat?

The Human Factors

Think time is an indispensable element in the creative process. Many famous people have written how this practice helped them become much more creative and effective. A good example is Albert Einstein, who took long walks so that he had time alone to think and refine his theories. More evidence can be found when you study breakthroughs, such as the invention of the semiconductor. Jack Kilby, the inventor, was relatively new to Texas Instruments when the breakthrough occurred. It was the middle of the summer, and he was almost alone at work because his coworkers were on vacation. This gave him plenty of think time, allowing the flash of brilliance about a silicon-based transistor to come to him. Because of the social environment, he was emotionally unflustered. One of the most significant inventions of this century arose out of a calm state of mind. People will say they are too busy to slow down, but the dividends quickly outweigh the costs. You just have to design think time into your organization's work routine. There is plenty of creativity if you let it flow.

> The key question isn't "What fosters creativity?" But why in God's name isn't everyone creative? Where was the human potential lost? How was it crippled? I think therefore a good question might not be why do people create? But why do people not create or innovate? We have got to abandon that sense of amazement in the face of creativity, as if it were a miracle that anybody created anything.
>
> —ABRAHAM MASLOW

The enthusiasm and creative energy freed when workers do what they love has great innovative value. These people have discovered their path, finding work closely aligned with their abilities. Because they enjoy their job, they often leave work thinking about a problem they are trying to solve, driven by passionate interest. It gives them great personal satisfaction to learn and excel. Individuals like this are more likely to create what you need, as long as the social environment doesn't shut them down.

Another technique that has been proven to work is to mix people with different points of view and thinking styles, à la Myers Briggs, which triggers creative abrasion, a well-documented method of stimulating group creativity. This was first noted by Jerry Hirshberg, founder and president of Nissan Design International. By having people with very different thinking styles, the mix of perspectives will produce new insights—once again, as long as the culture is supportive. If not, they will rub up against each other, creating negative friction and actually damaging your output.

Steve Jobs once said, "Creativity is just connecting things." He was right, but across much of corporate America, creativity is difficult to achieve because people lack experience, due either to downsizing that eliminated tenured workers or to jobs that were offshored to junior individuals with technical knowledge but little institutional knowledge. Because the offshore IT workers turn over at a rapid rate, experience remains limited. So, knowing which jobs are difficult to master and/or critical to your success and retaining them so you can nurture deep and intimate institutional knowledge among your staff is crucial to innovation. Only intimate experience provides a multitude of threads of knowledge to interconnect, driving innovation. I delve more deeply into this in Chapter 13.

You also get what you ask for. If you encourage your teams to be creative, reward it, and are a good audience, then more innovation will be expressed. Studies have shown that people respond positively to encouragement, *so seek and you shall find.*

Build a Culture of Creativity

Culturally, you will also want an open environment. If people are really valued, then their opinions count; encourage staff members to speak up freely and ensure they are listened to patiently. All too often, poor communicators are rudely interrupted, causing them to withdraw and feel they aren't valued for who they are. People have many gifts; even if they aren't great communicators, they may have incredible domain knowledge and the creativity to conceive a remarkable innovation. Build an accepting culture where people can comfortably be themselves, and you increase your odds of stimulating innovative capacity. Einstein said, "The important thing is to not stop questioning." If you don't have a culture where people feel comfortable to speak up, the important questions may never be asked, and the innovative insights will be lost.

History shows that closely connected individuals can create greatness, which leads me to believe there is a contagious element at work. These explosions of creativity have come in clusters, which shows that people feed on the knowledge and passion of others. The more creative your teams, the greater the likelihood innovation will be expressed. These flourishes of greatness have occurred when co-creators were supported within a social milieu that multiplied what each individual would have done operating alone.

There's a way to do it better—find it.

—THOMAS EDISON

There are a number of examples of these creative outbursts in recent history. We see a burst of passion and creativity across America's founding fathers in the 1700s, as they collectively changed the direction of the world by writing so coherently about democracy and the power of freedom; or we can look at the great cluster of German philosophers and physicists in the second half of the 1800s, who revolutionized thinking in philosophy and physics; or American inventors in the nineteenth century who brought about the era of industrialization. Beyond these, consider the Manhattan Project or, more recently, Silicon Valley and the PC revolution. What all of these have in common is a cluster of like-minded individuals who feed off of the collective consciousness. I'm by no means implying that you can achieve something of this magnitude; rather, you can unleash innovation if you create a supportive milieu and hire for creativity. Get these areas right and you will be very surprised how much can happen.

What does this mean for IT? Since IT is half art, it shares many creative properties with music. The desired state of your teams is to have the composers, and professionals in other creative roles such as system architecture, begin jamming together, united in a state of flow and harmony. This is the moment when the professionals are relaxed enough, open-minded enough, and emotionally tuned in enough to creatively remove barriers to progress on the fly and revel in the feeling that the creative dam has broken.

At this moment, a positive energy begins to grip people as they solve one problem after another and realize they are supercharged and in a state of "flow." Solutions pop into consciousness and can be clearly articulated, grasped, and internalized. The shared vision has emerged, and everyone begins to play off each other, in a way that was not possible prior to the common understanding that manifested itself through teamwork and open sharing within this emotionally safe environment. Strive to build this level of professional intimacy, and greatness can come out of it.

Also, don't forget to build a blame-free culture. Innovation is often about trying and failing. If failure becomes blame, you have an innovation short-circuit. If you can view mistakes as learning experiences, you are on the right track. Some companies encourage people to experiment so that they can continually come up with new products. These embrace the saying "We fail fast, often, and cheap."

Last, laughter and humor are great aids to creativity and therefore innovation. Encourage people to have fun. By so doing, you will get more creativity and a lot more productivity, too.

In my experience, the best creative work is never done when one is unhappy.

—ALBERT EINSTEIN

I've covered a list of actions you should incorporate into your design. But don't try to quantify the value of each driver. Build the right culture, and innovation will come. At that point, innovation can express itself and even flourish, *enabling almost anything to happen*. Imagine that.

You may feel you need to augment the staff you have with talent that is not just creative but capable of creating innovation in specific areas. This requires you to add domain-specific technical experience to your talent mix. If you have that need, you can plan for it and build that into your workforce plan. We take a look at this process in Chapter 13.

Workforce Planning

*Maximizing the Productivity of
Your Talent—Today and Tomorrow*

Tell me and I forget.
Teach me and I remember.
Involve me and I learn.

—BENJAMIN FRANKLIN

The dehumanization of the workforce has produced many negative consequences, for both corporations and knowledge workers. I have covered these extensively throughout this book. The prior chapters focused on how to *manage* the workforce better by applying the human factors of productivity; this chapter focuses on how to *plan* it.

Corporate America thinks short term. In fact, the planning horizon often does not extend beyond the next quarter. One of the most significant problems with this short-term bias is the negative effect it has on the growth and development of the workforce. Add to this the notion that professionals are just replaceable parts, and management is absolved of responsibility to care deeply about its workers. This explains why workforce planning is missing in most companies. Organizations remain tactically focused on short-term project staffing needs, choosing to be reactive rather than proactive. In addition, many have embraced a commodity view of labor, looking for the cheapest parts, not the most productive and talented ones.

But this is way off the mark. Information technology (IT) is a talent business, more than anything else. Winning companies acquire and grow the best talent, letting it fully express itself within supportive cultures and work environments. Yes, there are some commodity roles, the natural by-product of any maturing industry. And this is a good thing. It enables you to focus on the talent that will differentiate your business. Workforce planning is a continuous cycle, because it is done year after year. This leads to the constant refinement

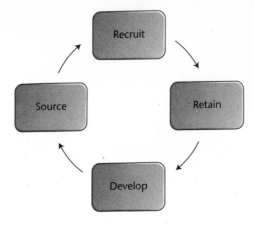

Figure 13.1   Talent Cycle

of your workforce, based on an ongoing reassessment of your recruiting and staff development needs, as shown in Figure 13.1.

Workforce planning is about recruiting, growing, and optimizing the talent that supports the evolution of your core business systems and infrastructure and at the same time putting programs in place to retain your key workers. Professionals aren't commodities; they never were. Complex jobs require intimate knowledge and creativity. To flourish, workers must be tightly woven into the fabric of your organization, sharing intimate knowledge of one another, and the business, seamlessly exchanging passion and understanding among themselves. As they share and support one another, social capital grows, quickening the pace of work and delivering higher returns on human capital. Implement this planning cycle fully, and the capability of your workforce will grow continuously, driving productivity to unimagined levels.

Given this, your goal is to build *high-aptitude teams* that are small, tight, deeply knowledgeable, efficient, and socially cohesive. That is the most productive structure you can create. But we must eliminate the gap first.

Workforce Planning Gap

The lack of workforce planning and, at a larger level, career planning that enables people to find what they are good at, has created an enormous disconnect in our society. In May 2012, the STAR Act (Securing the Talent America Requires for the 21st Century Act of 2012) was introduced into the Senate by John Cornyn (R-Texas), to make green cards, or permanent residency, available to 55,000 foreign students who earn an advanced degree, either a master's or PhD, from a research university (a university that receives federal funding for research). I applaud the legislation, and believe America should continue to attract and retain the top professionals in the world. Having great talent, and creating an environment where it can flourish, enables businesses to form and grow, expanding opportunities in the society. So, keeping great talent that was trained in our universities by making green cards available is economically sensible.

That said, we need to make technology careers attractive for our own youth again. During the dot-com boom, computer science professors had to turn prospective students away because of overenrollment, only to find that, from 2000 to 2007, enrollment declined. A new upturn began in 2008, "as U.S. undergraduate enrollment in computer science rose 8.1%."[1] Sounds encouraging, but "in 2009 the U.S. only graduated 37,994 students with bachelor's degrees in computer and information science. When you examine the statistics, you find we graduated more students with computer science degrees 25 years ago!"[2] At that point, the distributed computing revolution had barely gotten under way, and the Internet revolution lay a decade ahead.

Today, IT remains a very attractive career, with top salaries for experienced professionals, but one consequence of our short-term, commodity-based thinking is that foreign talent sees it as a pathway to success and works hard to earn their degrees, ultimately coming here and launching impressive careers. Because we have failed to embrace our domestic talent, our youth is looking elsewhere for opportunity. Clearly, America needs to do a better job.

Furthermore, the biggest beneficiaries of workforce planning are the corporations themselves, so the opportunity to reverse these trends must originate here. Talent is the pathway to competitive advantage. Our corporations will benefit the most by embracing workforce planning as a tool. An incredible number of people have the aptitude to do this work right here, and we need to build feeder systems to tap this talent and bring them into corporations where they can excel, just as those Americans that invented and built the IT industry did. To win, companies must build high-performing teams that are woven into the fabric of their organization, highly motivated, sharing both a mission and a purpose. What is outlined in this book, and chapter, will help them achieve that. At a time when so many qualified people are looking for a good job, highly educated talent is abundant and available.

Throughout this book I have clearly shown that acquiring great talent is a priority. It must be recruited, nurtured, wired into your culture, and given the opportunity to acquire deep and meaningful institutional experience so it can fully express its productive potential. Talented, high-aptitude professionals are not a commodity; they never were. It is time for corporations to see the wisdom behind workforce planning. People count. They always have. Building a talented workforce must start within corporate America. Today we are too focused on the short term and have neglected long-term talent strategy. Clearly, we should plan our talent needs as well as we plan our hardware refreshes.

Goals and Process

You will need to communicate simple, understandable goals for your workforce planning initiative. Ultimately, this is a core governance process that needs to become part of the fabric of your organization. It should be treated just like the budgeting, planning, and performance management processes. My recommendation is to keep the goals very simple, so they are easy to remember, with a logical flow that makes the benefits obvious.

At a high level, consider these goals, which I have used as a CIO:

- Recruit the best and the brightest.
- Develop them.
- Retain them.
- Utilize both domestic and offshore consulting companies in the right roles for the right tasks.
- Build the leaders of tomorrow.
- Drive increasing productivity.
- Position IT for the future.

Simplicity is much more powerful than complexity.

The high-level process is also simple, as you can see in Figure 13.2.

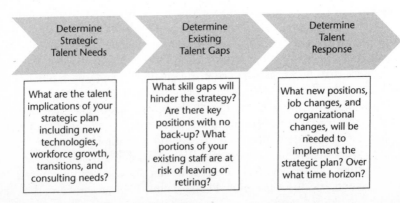

Figure 13.2 Workforce Planning Process

Workforce planning is proactive while project staffing is reactive; it is informed by your multiyear strategic plan and emerging challenges, such as the demographics of your organization (demographics are destiny); it provides an accurate forecast of your needs, now and into the future; it enables you to give a prioritized staffing plan to your talent acquisition team; it allows you to confidently build a feeder system with universities and training schools; ultimately, it ensures you are building the next generation of talent for your company.

Sometimes leaders push back, saying they don't have time to work on something as comprehensive as workforce planning. My retort always was "This is your job." At the same time, it is important to realize that perfecting a workforce plan is a multiyear process. It takes time to build mature processes, so plan on phasing pieces of them in. Different departments can focus on specific needs based on their immediate challenges. Some might be working on new and emerging technology and have a need to plan for what is coming over a two-year horizon; another area might be faced with aging demographics and need to plan for that instead. The key is making workforce planning a priority and attacking it in an organized fashion. Every area should schedule time to plan its staffing needs and not fall prey to the tactical project work that presses in on them. Those day-to-day pressures will always be there.

Context Diagram

Workforce planning is a set of interconnected activities that ideally should be cycled through once a year. It makes sense to combine workforce planning with your strategic and annual planning processes, to identify precisely what your short- and long-term staffing needs are.

Let's look at each of the pieces in Figure 13.3.

The *IT strategic plan* should have a three-year horizon, with complete detail for the coming year and less for the out years. This plan must be aligned with the enterprise strategy and each line of business. Based on your immediate and longer-term needs, you can identify where you have to increase capacity, augment staff temporarily for large initiatives, or plan on building expertise to support a new or emerging technology. Net-net, this is the basis of your workforce strategy.

One thing many companies have to plan for is the changing mix of systems from in-house to cloud. As you increase the use of software as a service (SaaS) applications or cloud infrastructure, the need to build software decreases, while you require more vendor management, more people who understand the nuances of negotiating a cloud contract, and more people who can execute a SaaS project life cycle. This life cycle is weighted toward system configuration, integration, and testing rather than construction. By analyzing your strategy, you will see demand for resources with these skills

Figure 13.3   Workforce Planning Cycle

increase over time, so you can now grow/acquire them gradually. Being proactive always yields better results.

Emerging technologies, or the introduction of a new technology into your company, will necessitate developing in-house expertise, unless you are outsourcing it to a partner. There are many entry points across applications and infrastructure, so each manager will need his or her own plan, built looking at both the present and the future. Often money is tight, so you can't be as forward looking in your actions as your plans, but you certainly can assign one of your existing people an additional role that requires them to start developing expertise in an important area.

With the aging of the baby boomers, *workforce demographics* and *knowledge transfer* are considerations for many companies, especially given the rich institutional knowledge these individuals have acquired over many, many years. Clearly, this is not an issue at some companies, but for those who have to contend with it, working closely with human resources (HR) to look at your staff demographics by business system or operational function is very important. Where you have emerging risks, you can build a formal process for transferring the knowledge. There are many ways to do this, but as long as you are proactively thinking about it, you can put the required actions into your plan.

Succession planning has been a traditional HR process for leadership roles for many years, but this hasn't been the case for technical roles. If your company has a mature process, leverage it fully and expand it to the technical ranks if currently out of scope. Knowing who your high-potential talent is, cultivating it, and calibrating a consistent view of who these people are across your department is critical, as is filling gaps by acquiring external talent. You should maintain a mix of junior, experienced, and senior resources on your key systems. At all times, you should be able to control your destiny for every core business system. If it sounds idealistic because of the financial pressures you face, I fully understand. What makes sense will vary from company to company based on the pressures you have to contend with. However, you can take small steps so you are not standing still, paralyzed by inaction. All of the input gathered needs to be consolidated, prioritized, and put into a succession plan showing what talent is needed, and when.

The next step is *sourcing* the talent. This process will include entry-level positions, experienced talent, consultants, and outsourced functions/roles. Your sourcing goal should be to acquire the best and brightest talent possible, as aptitude is the number one driver of productivity. Track record really matters. You want a strong bench and people who can grow with your company. Take this seriously, as mistakes are very costly, in both time and money. No matter what you do, hiring mistakes happen, but the wisdom of crowds will help you avert many wrong hires, so avoid relying on one person's opinion. People should be free to speak up, and no one should be able to railroad their favorite person through the hiring process, as this is where many bad fits come from.

You will also have to build *feeder systems* by working with universities and key consulting partners. Many body shops go into the market to acquire talent for you, but all of these firms, unless they have their own employees, are fishing in the same pool. As you build your vendor list, add companies that have pools of vertical expertise that are not available anywhere else. Doing this will give you access to some really good talent, and it is worth it, even if these resources cost more. Building talent takes time, but can you afford not to? Even if you don't do it immediately, make it part of the plan, and gradually assemble it. Since the goal is productivity, you should use consultants in the right roles, for the right tasks. Consultants working on projects in-house should come, do their work, and go. Many firms have clear policies on how long a consultant can be on an assignment, but an equal number do not.

Lastly, you are going to want to retain your talent. If you work for a healthy company, and follow what has been covered previously in this book, retention will not be an issue. People leave because they are not appreciated, and if you care for them, show them empathy and compassion, and build high levels of trust, the good ones will stay. Make sure your HR processes are fair, and employ all the human factors. My turnover was always very low. Yours can be, too.

Outsourcing and Offshoring

> While this 10 to 1 productivity differential among programmers is understandable, there is also a 10 to 1 difference in productivity among software organizations.
>
> —HARLAN MILLS

The inability to measure productivity has created many damaging trends in IT, including offshoring support for critical business systems. There are many tools in IT, and outsourcing/offshoring is one of them. I am not anti-offshoring, but, like any tool, it needs to be used right. How should you approach this area?

Peter Drucker got it right when he said the most valuable assets of a twenty-first-century company would be its knowledge workers. They *are* assets. And, as he rightly pointed out, as assets, they must be grown. So, the key to intelligently outsourcing/offshoring functions is to understand which roles are assets and which roles are expenses. You can do that by determining what roles are true commodities.

IT is a talent game, and there are enormous differences between the competency of top talent and average talent. Based on research done back in the 1970s and 1980s, top programmers, for instance, are 10 times more productive than average ones (see end note 8 in Chapter 1). This profession requires aptitude, and it is no different from sports, where the best players are just so much better, they stand out. Clearly, you want individuals with high aptitude and deep experience. Aptitude and experience drive productivity. That's a fact.

In addition, as discussed in the last chapter, you need people with diverse knowledge and experience to innovate anything. The greater the knowledge and the tighter the social cohesion, the greater your innovation potential. Absent innovation, your company will slowly die, as it liquidates its assets year over year, either through competitive encroachment or by replacing highly capable assets (great talent) with cheap commodity labor. I see many companies doing that today. Revenues are stagnant, but profits are growing, because they are reducing expenses. That's great, as long as you are not simply mortgaging your future by replacing highly productive assets with unproductive ones, and cheering as this liquidation process produces an earnings spike. It is not sustainable.

When you have incredible talent that is a good cultural fit working for you, it is evident immediately. Their brains are wired perfectly for this business, so they learn complex systems quickly and come up with brilliant solutions to problems. Every day that goes by, they become more intimately familiar with your business systems, the culture, and your strategy. Their institutional knowledge and social competence grow, driving up their productivity.

This productivity growth is directly related to the level of complexity that must be mastered. Complex systems have millions of lines of instruction, involved architectures, and multiple software products woven into them. These are incredibly intricate puzzles to unravel and grasp, but some brains work through the complexity very fast. The same can be said about becoming a tightly knit member of the social fabric. Both take caring, aptitude, and time; the time represents the investment the company makes so individuals can acquire institutional experience and social capital. This then brings up the notion of time to competency.

You cannot create experience. You must undergo it.

—ALBERT CAMUS

Time to competency is a learning model first developed by Noel Burch of Gordon Training International in the 1970s, and Figure 13.4 is adapted from his original work. As a concept it is extremely valuable for IT, because the learning curve can go from days to years. Systems are very complex to understand, and if you have ever tried to take over an application and modify it, as I have, you know how daunting it can be to unravel the logic puzzle and learn the business function. Gifted technicians were much quicker than I.

For this discussion, imagine a complex system, with two million lines of instruction, multiple complex databases, and a code base that has been modified by many different brains, each of which applies different "brushstrokes," adding to the complexity. Let's assume the average time to full competency is two years for someone with the aptitude to grasp the whole application (many never do). Here is how their learning progresses and how their productivity increases.

When you assign people to a system, they don't know the scope and size of the application. At this point, they are *unconsciously incompetent*, with

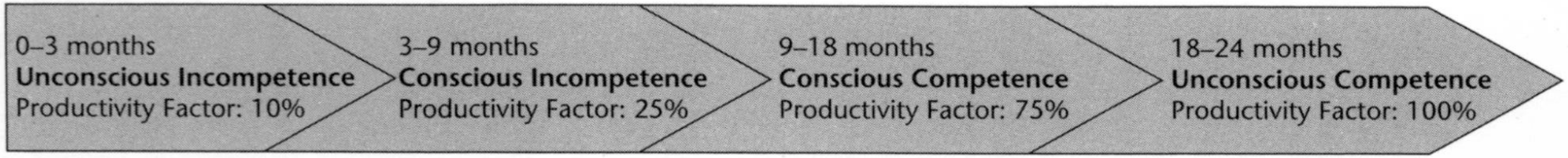
0–3 months
Unconscious Incompetence
Productivity Factor: 10%
3–9 months
Conscious Incompetence
Productivity Factor: 25%
9–18 months
Conscious Competence
Productivity Factor: 75%
18–24 months
Unconscious Competence
Productivity Factor: 100%

Figure 13.4 Time to Competency
Source: Adapted from work by Gordon Training International

essentially no institutional knowledge and no feel for how much they don't know. Each day they work on the system their understanding grows, but they are still highly dependent on the subject matter experts. Generally, they will be assigned to one area of the application, and they will master that while they begin to understand the big picture: the number of major domains, the over-arching business function(s), their teammates, how to navigate the system, and so on. Their productivity will go from 0 percent to perhaps 10 percent. Since their knowledge is still limited, at the end of three months, they can be assigned work within a narrow area.

At three months, and it varies by system based on complexity, they become conscious of all they don't know. Now they are *consciously incompetent*, and this dawning of awareness motivates most professionals to fill their knowledge gaps. Learning picks up, because they understand the full context and can begin to learn in an organized fashion. Productivity grows, assuming they have the aptitude. If they don't, a good manager will already sense that they do not comprehend the material and will start to watch them more closely, eventually replacing them if they don't achieve a mental breakthrough. At the end of nine months, they may be only 25 percent productive, but they now have more intimate knowledge and can begin to make connections faster, because they have a broader basis of understanding. At this point, they are working more independently, and learning picks up speed.

Next they move to the *consciously competent* phase. They know multiple domains and can be assigned work on just about any part of the system, because they are quickly unraveling new portions of the application. Produc-tivity goes up, so they are now 50 to 75 percent productive, on a relative basis. The system architecture is now clear, although areas of the system remain a black box. Eventually, they will work on those as well, becoming masters.

The last phase emerges when they have unraveled the puzzle fully. At this point they have such detailed knowledge and understanding, they are *unconsciously competent*. Their understanding has become second nature, fully internalized, so they are able to work very fast, a true expert, consulted by others on the team.

However, there is an incredible range of competency potential across resources. All of this is a rule of thumb, totally dependent on your mix of tal-ent. A year is a significant investment of capital for someone to learn a job. If the average is a year, someone with high aptitude may be able to master it in six months, while someone lacking the aptitude will take two years to achieve mediocrity—or never grasp it at all. This is the mythical man-month that Frederick Brooks wrote about 45 years ago. Not much has changed since he wrote about this topic. In the IT business, an unconsciously competent star can solve a highly complex problem in five minutes that an incompetent per-son might analyze for a month to find a solution (notice the use of the word *a*, because the solution might be a poor one even then). Which matters: the cost per hour of labor or the productivity of the resource? It's clear productivity is the driver, just as it always has been in business. We have lost total sight of this in IT in this country.

When you are considering offshoring part of your application portfolio, time to competency is a key driver of return on investment. You lose complete control over the application, no longer growing competency by finding the best and brightest and retaining them so their institutional knowledge grows, along with their output. If you have offshored/outsourced something, and the workers are turning over quickly, as is most often the case, the individuals assigned to your business systems are in the first two phases of competency *forever*. That is just so unproductive, based on the facts. The fact that we have yet to design a measurement system for knowledge worker productivity does not mean it is not real and a key consideration. Ignore it at your company's peril—and yours as well.

In one instance in my career, our offshore partner had very high turnover and had over 50 people assigned to support a complex system. The executive in charge of IT for that line of business began growing a high-aptitude team. The 50 offshore resources were replaced by a team of 6 people, and productivity, by every measure tracked, went up a lot. We had been paying for churn. Most people have lost the intimate knowledge and understanding of their applications and make a business case by comparing two different resources, claiming they are identical. If they were measuring productivity instead, the answer would change. During my entire career in this business, small teams of gifted people do the highest-quality work, and at the lowest price. Why? They are high aptitude and can quickly share information to achieve conceptual unity. These teams offer both speed and accuracy.

Every organization should develop a clear strategy for what it keeps and what it uses a partner for. So, to offshore, or not to offshore: That is the question.

Here's a model for deciding:

1. **If the system is core to your business, retain intellectual control, if not full control**. I would have a core team of unconsciously competent people who direct all work on the system and oversee anything done by a partner (if you choose to augment your staff with offshore help). These highly competent professionals are there to maintain the integrity of the application and make sure that all work conforms to the underlying architecture. They ensure that the significant investment made to build the application isn't destroyed by inexperienced people who try hard but make uninformed decisions. Poor decisions literally degrade the "tightness" of the application, making future

efforts more difficult, more costly, less productive, and shortening the usable life of the solution.

Another reason you want intellectual control is to make sure every estimate is fair, based on what it would take someone competent to do the work. In one of my turnarounds, a lot of business had been outsourced, and a complex contract governed all work. The vendor's account executive approached me and said it needed to run year-end tax reporting and filing, and it wasn't part of the contract. The change order was for 5,000 hours of work, and he assumed I would just sign it, because every competent technician had been replaced. Fortunately, I intimately knew what it took to execute year-end processing, because we ran the same package at my prior company. Based on my years of experience, it was a few hundred hours at most.

I said, "I'm not signing it. Based on my experience, your estimate is 10 times what I believe it costs to do this. Bring me a detailed estimate of every task, each one no more than 5 hours in duration, and we will review them task by task to get to a mutually agreeable cost." The final change order was 400 hours, which was still high but reasonable. Had I not had intimate knowledge, the 5,000-hour charge would have been signed and paid for.

That is exactly what was happening before I arrived. Needless to say, I began immediately rebuilding the institutional knowledge that had been lost. Companies without institutional knowledge are highly exposed to what I refer to as "stickups." Unfortunately, this is occurring all over corporate America because the value of institutional knowledge was neither understood nor appreciated. If we had human capital accounting, the true costs and risks would be known, and the business cases would not make sense.

2. **If you have a platform that is in maintenance mode because no new products are being added, get a less expensive team off-shore to maintain it.** The platform is no longer strategic to your business, and your strong talent needs to be working on important projects and systems. This is a great opportunity to move expenses from run-the-business to invest-in-the-business, by lowering non-value added support costs.

3. **Production support teams, covering nightly production when it is daytime for them, work very well.** Your teams can sleep and refresh themselves, and the business keeps running. This is a great benefit to the IT organization. The competency of the offshore team drives the amount of involvement when problems are encountered.

The higher the level of competence, the more sleep teams here can get.

4. **If you have a function with short time to competency, it makes sense to use commodity labor.** A good example of this is configuring a Windows 2010 server or a Unix server. The work is almost the same across every company. This function is a true commodity. You should retain control of your configuration standards, but you can hire the actual labor very cheaply offshore. The function adds no strategic value but needs to be done. A small core of highly skilled workers can provide oversight and ensure that the security model is maintained by reviewing and approving all configuration changes, keeping the configuration standards up to date, and helping design future ones. Last, move to automated provisioning, and eliminate the resources completely.

5. **If you are doing something innovative, build a team of creative people and create a supportive climate (see Chapter 14).** Offshore is a leverage model, with lots of bodies thrown at problems and projects. These staffing models are not innovative.

Anything can be commoditized, literally. When the output is something you can see, touch, and feel, everyone grasps the difference between a creative person's work, and a non-creative person's work. A product built by someone with deep aptitude and passion is immediately visible.

I often think how dreadful movies would be if we used the same commodity labor model we use for IT to create them. Imagine a producer saying, "I need a team of writers, a director with three years' experience, a cinematographer, and six actors, one of whom will be the lead. And they better be great. We really need a hit at the box office."

Guess what? No one would go to see those films, the critics would pan them, and it would be evident the casting model was cheap but ineffective. Talent is not a commodity; it never was and never will be. IT will continue to fail at unacceptable rates until management addresses the talent and leadership practices that have gotten us here. Given all this, building a high-aptitude team takes time. A great staff is built over many years by thoughtfully filtering through team members, with those who are below average moving on. People without the required aptitude are replaced with qualified personnel; individuals who don't fit into the mix are replaced with people who are socially cohesive with the team; people who are not committed to the mission normally opt out on their own, or fail; people who haven't found their way move on. Eventually, you have a team with high aptitude and deep institutional experience who collaborate in an open and meaningful way and who can maintain the architectural integrity of the software because they are intimately familiar with it. I'm not suggesting a team of all-stars—that just doesn't work; but one that is well balanced, with a high aptitude quotient—no question. If you get there, and your culture is supportive, you will have the model fully operational, as shown in Figure 13.5.

Once you have built a great team, you need to hang on to it. Teams take time to build and refine, so each one is a corporate asset. Much of this book is devoted to building a highly productive work environment. To do this, leaders need to focus time on career development, career pathing, showing appreciation, and caring about their professionals by providing work–life balance; they need to ensure the work has meaning, provide recognition, and build a prosocial, supportive social environment. This will keep your retention high. At every company I joined, I built a culture where the employees mattered, and turnover dropped to the low single digits within a year. It's not hard to accomplish.

If you plan your workforce right and build a great culture, your organization will flourish, as will productivity. It's been studied many times.

Our study found that there were huge differences between the 92 competing organizations. Over the whole sample, the best organization worked 11.1 times faster than the worst organization.

—Tom DeMarco and Timothy Lister

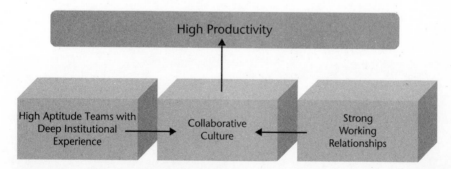

Figure 13.5   Model for High Productivity

If your organization was studied, where would it fit on the curve?

I have spent a lot of time on how the human factors drive productivity, so the question is, how do you take this information and apply it where you work? Chapter 14 provides a framework that will enable you to tie this all together, including what IT best practices matter.

Notes

1. Carolyn Duffy Marsan, "Computer Science Major Is Cool Again," *Network World*, March 17, 2009. Available at www.networkworld.com/news/2009/031409-computer-science-majors .html.
2. Alex Tabarrok, "College Has Been Oversold," Marginal Revolution Blog, November 2, 2011. Available at http://marginalrevolution.com/marginalrevolution/2011/11/college-has-been -oversold.html.

CHAPTER 14

How to Successfully Transform Your Organization

Putting It All Together

Your work is going to fill a large part of your life, and the only way to be truly satisfied is to do what you believe is great work. And the only way to do great work is to love what you do. If you haven't found it yet, keep looking. Don't settle. As with all matters of the heart, you'll know when you find it. And, like any great relationship, it just gets better and better as the years roll on. So keep looking until you find it. Don't settle.

—STEVE JOBS

I really like this quote. Many people have said the equivalent of love what you do and never work a day in your life. Jobs's quote is more eloquent, but the sentiment is just so true. For me, information technology (IT) has been fascinating and I have enjoyed my career, and still do. Where else can you get paid to turn concepts into reality; creatively leverage technology to solve business problems; adapt to rapid and constant change; work with so many deeply intelligent, fun, and interesting people; regularly overcome significant challenges; and be given responsibility for a big staff and critically important initiatives?

It has been a great career, and I was fortunate to enter the profession when we relied on a mainframe and punch cards, so I have seen it evolve through many incredible generations of technology, bringing us to a hyperconnected era where IT solutions have become the nervous system and half the brain of almost every company. I love the business and have learned an immense amount about technology and collaborative social systems—the human infrastructure—ultimately being selected to drive complex turnaround transformations.

As in everything, experience matters, and there are strategies and tactics that will enable you to excel at IT leadership. That said, this book is predominantly about transforming IT culture in order to maximize your return on talent. But to successfully transform your culture, you not only have to get the human infrastructure working, you also have to apply IT best practices. In this last chapter, I am going to delve into IT transformation more broadly so that you have a blueprint for success.

Here are some thoughts based on my experience, in the form of an outline that will help you transform your organization. You can shape this outline to meet your specific needs, because success is *always situational*. There is no one-size-fits-all magic formula. Great outcomes are the result of insightful artistic expression that ensures your strategy and design fit the corporate canvas you are working on. Companies excel at some things while lagging behind in others. Enterprise-wide programs exist that you will need to harmonize with; there are strategic imperatives and a history of decisions evident in the residue left behind—both good and bad; all of this must be taken into account, so measure twice and cut once. You must consider every dimension as you evaluate what needs to be accomplished, the best tactics to employ, and the timing. Normally, fixing the human infrastructure gives you the biggest leverage. As I always say, *you fix IT one interaction at a time*.

The human factors that drive great IT, as outlined in this book, are absolutely critical. You must focus on this as talent is around two thirds of your operating costs, and the source of competitive advantage. IT failure is driven by social pathologies that lead to protective behaviors, disengagement, weak social cohesion, silos, walls, ignorance of the human factors, and antisocial behaviors; treating people like interchangeable parts leads to low levels of institutional knowledge, errors, and costly projects. In environments like this, whole teams can burn through a lot of money going through the motions.

In contrast, a high-aptitude professional, deeply engaged in his or her work, with deep institutional experience, can be a team of one. A brilliant mind that intimately understands a large domain of knowledge has instant access to all of it, solves problems quickly, and also knows how to correctly evolve the system as the business changes. Yes, one great mind can be a whole team, but only if you acquire, cultivate, and nurture it. Focus a lot of your up-front time on the human factors.

Great IT is the product of many designs: governance, organization, culture, workforce, process, operations, and technical (network, hardware, and software). Each design needs to be thoughtfully approached and woven together. We look briefly at each of these.

Also, no matter what you focus on, remain vigilant about minimizing complexity. While not always top of mind for IT executives, reducing complexity drives improvements in speed and resiliency. Complexity increases costs and lowers productivity; it makes the learning curve steeper, increases the number of specialized skills required to run your organization, and limits your flexibility; and it is strongly correlated with poor operational reliability. If you need to drive improvement in your operational uptime, reducing complexity across your technology stack will help you attain your goals, with a lower total cost.

So, fix the human infrastructure, limit complexity, and try to make things simple. Albert Einstein was right when he said that people should "make everything as simple as possible, but not simpler." Let's take a look at how you can do that.

High-Level Outline

An overarching approach is as simple as this:

- Choose an efficient organizational design.
- Communicate a clear strategy.
- Set the right tone at the top.
- Recruit and retain the best talent.
- Design a culture where talent flourishes.
- Cultivate rich institutional experience.
- Leverage IT best practices.
- Win over the hearts and minds of the business.

Although the approach is simple, IT itself has many complexities. Never underestimate your adversary. Rome wasn't built in a day, so a key success factor is intelligently phasing these steps in; trying to do too much at the outset leads to failure, just when credibility is your most important currency. You may not get a second chance if you try to do too much and fail. The fact that you reached far will neither be seen nor appreciated. When you become chief information officer (CIO), you are likely reporting to someone who really doesn't know what you do because IT is a career, and you can't become a practitioner through observation. Consequently, if you reach for the moon by pursuing a very complex set of objectives, observers have no feel for *how far you reached*, because IT is experiential. So, try to do as much as you can, *but no more*. Adjust the tempo and pace as you get a feel for the capabilities of the professionals under you and how cohesive the organization is.

Organizational Design

You have three choices on how to organize: centralized, decentralized, and federated. How your company operates and what the firm's strategy is will define what organizational model you choose. In general, you have to achieve a balance between autonomy and synergy, with shared services driving the synergy and independent action driving the desire for autonomy. This balance is seen in both domestic and global companies. Generally, the greater the synergy, the greater the required collaboration; if you shoot for synergy yet lack a collaborative culture, progress stagnates as local needs and the desire for control overshadow collaborative actions.

I have seen corporations move from centralized to decentralized models over time. When the need to optimize expenses is paramount, a shared service structure provides a way to remove redundancy and lower the cost of service; when speed is paramount, independent action unfettered by a central bureaucracy becomes more attractive. The movement back and forth removes power from entrenched bureaucracies that become self-serving and stifling to navigate as they project power through complex processes. At times it makes sense to leave areas decentralized, especially if they may be spun off later.

From a strictly IT perspective, the most useful organizational design is one that is federated across two dimensions: business and IT. Building a deep relationship with the business and breaking down the walls is greatly aided by an organizational matrix. In Figure 14.1, the departmental CIOs are federated into both IT and the business such that each departmental CIO has a seat at the business and IT tables, so he or she can look out for the best interest of the business while still being an integral member of the IT senior leadership team.

Deep collaboration is required to get anything done in IT, and as complexity, integration, and hyperspecialization grow, such collaboration becomes even more critical. You must work hard to break down the walls, silos, and cubicles, freeing the flow of information and building relationships. To achieve this across divisions, my line-of-business CIOs were matrixed, and at the same time, all IT projects became jointly owned, with both business and IT sharing the outcome. This method established a sound framework for collaboration and ensured we

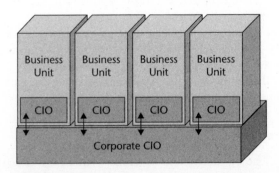

Figure 14.1   Federated IT: CIO Matrix

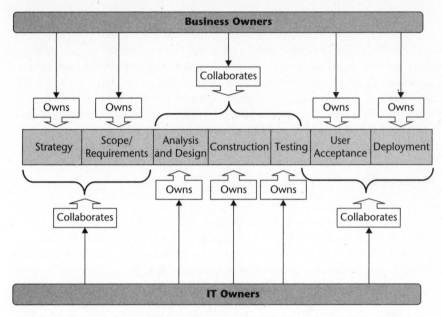

Figure 14.2 Project Collaboration by Design

didn't have IT projects but *business* projects. After all, technology solutions are simply the automated portion of the business's processes and products, so anything other than joint ownership is artificial. A certain amount of failure is baked right in if you don't federate. The operational model for managing projects looks like Figure 14.2.

From the IT side of the federation, the business always wants its costs decreasing based on an agreed-on metric (e.g., percentage of revenue). Migrating to a shared services structure reduces operating expenses, which lowers their chargebacks. IT itself is structured horizontally, but systems are built on a vertical technology stack (application, services, databases, hardware). This means that systems are a shared responsibility of the application and infrastructure areas, since both own pieces of the solution. To run effectively, a high level of collaboration and shared ownership between every area within IT is indispensable. A shared services model helps deepen collaboration, as long as there is a supportive culture.

Since the business and customer are always paramount, I also like to use a plan, build, run paradigm. Doing this helps create role clarity within IT by providing a simple model against which to assign organizational roles while clearly establishing service relationships. The shared services areas support IT, with some business touch points, while the CIOs support the business and sales. It is paramount that the businesses have someone from within IT looking out for their best interests, ensuring they are getting the right solutions at the right price. You must make sure the service relationships are clear, so there is one person/area that owns the client relationship, even though others, such as desktop, provide support. The owner must be the departmental CIO, who has a seat at the business table because of the matrix. The CIO is fully supported by shared services, which is an internal-facing organization that provides IT-to-IT and IT-to-business services.

From a service relationship perspective, the model looks like Figure 14.3.

Strategy

Strategy is key, because if you have the right strategy, you will end up in the right place, even if there is a detour along the way. You must remain tuned in to where the company is going, and be an active listener. The most urgent needs are always put on the table, so bake them into the strategy right up front. If you listen, the approach will become clear. People are not bashful about expressing their needs.

In order to establish clean strategic phasing, I normally approach transformations in three overlapping phases: stabilize, optimize, and transform, as shown in Figure 14.4. This construct is an easily understood way to position the strategy with the business and upper management. However, when dealing

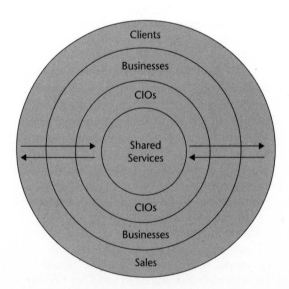

Figure 14.3   Service Relationships

with IT, I found it was helpful to highlight the phases as walk, hustle, and run. This structure resonated in IT because it was less formal, was lively, and conveyed a very clear message: We are going to work hard, and it is okay to have some fun. Research has shown that keeping it light is a great aid to creativity and collaboration, both of which are enormously helpful when you are on a challenging mission. This nomenclature also showed how speed would pick up as we moved forward and also made it clear that we were starting slowly and thoughtfully because getting it right was imperative. A headlong rush forward wasn't going to serve anyone's needs, least of all those of our division.

Figure 14.4 is illustrative. What you actually do and how you do it is based entirely on your situation. But the methodology is simple to convey and easily understood. Remember, humans have limited working memory, so keep the number of variables easy to digest.

Tone

Tone is powerful, so creating a positive, collaborative and prosocial tone up, down, and across the organization is highly beneficial. We know that managers are transmitters while employees are the receivers. As demonstrated earlier in the book, research into the dynamics of social hierarchy clearly shows the contagious nature of mood and behavior—and almost everyone has witnessed this contagion in action. Embrace this notion, explain why it is important to every leader, and be a positive beacon.

Stabilize/Walk	Optimize/Hustle	Transform/Run
Culture	Governance I	Technology Strategy
Talent	Real Collaboration	Metric-Based Management
Availability	Joint Ownership	Governance II
Organization and Roles	Expense Optimization	Expense Transformation
Execution	Full Federation	Innovation
Trust	Deepen Relationships	Information Management
Credibility	Role Clarity	Enterprise Strategies

Figure 14.4   Strategy Phasing: Conceptual Model

From your very first day on the job, let your positive mood, confidence, and caring bias state loudly who you are. If you have to tell people who you are, you have already failed. Your mood and behaviors are open books that everyone around you is reading and absorbing. The greater your reach and control, the more steadying and impactful your mood must be. Hopefully you can do this naturally, but if not, practice. If you need a moment to vent, go into your office behind closed door or take a walk to release the negative energy.

Since people don't do what you say but rather do what you do, model the right behaviors and communicate exactly what you are going to do, how you are going to do it, and how important the right culture and collaboration are to achieving success. Talk about your strategy and how building credibility is absolutely imperative. Also, make clear that IT is not an island: Every project must be a business project, even if it only involves technology. There is always a business reason, even if it is as simple as reducing operational risk; there *has* to be one for a project to take place. Technology projects have a high degree of failure, so make sure everything you do is about the business, is jointly owned by business and IT, and is understood by all.

Last, if you are a leader, make sure you are a servant. There is no need to tell your folks you are one; it will be perfectly clear to everyone. If you transmit a selfish tone, everyone will become more selfish, short-circuiting much-needed collaboration. Care about your teams and the people you work with. Nothing speaks louder.

Talent

Talent is, and remains, the only shortcut. Nothing is more important than hiring talent. But building a great workforce takes time, so talent is grown and acquired in phases, beginning with stabilization. Have your leaders identify every key position (the assets), including all single points of failure (no backup), and fill them with the best talent you can find. For example, hire consultants already working in your organization with proven track records and deep institutional knowledge, and source excellent talent from a willing market. By filling critical gaps with employees, you ensure that project investments create products and services and intimate institutional knowledge.

Once you have the key spots filled, move toward workforce planning. As reviewed in detail in Chapter 13, getting the right mix of talent is both a tactical exercise and a strategic one. Since the right strategy will come as relationships, talent, and understanding grow, workforce planning won't develop fully until you have stabilized and optimized your organization.

Also build strong relationships with your talent acquisition organization and key suppliers of talent. Doing this should be part of your vendor management strategy, because vendors often specialize by building great pools of talent that are available only through them. Many of the best people are not available any other way, so these vendors are an important source of supply that needs to be cultivated and worked over time.

Culture

Much of this book has been devoted to the topic of culture. Since you are designing the culture from the ground up, everything you do must result in deeper collaboration, higher levels of trust, and more fluid interaction. As noted in Chapter 1, you want to ensure that trust, collaboration, sharing, empathy, compassion, selflessness, prosocial behavior, harmony, openness, acceptance, mutual respect, and transparency are freely flowing within a blame-free culture. Communicate, communicate, and communicate again the need for every one of these cultural goals to be embraced and take hold. At first, people will agree, but they will hesitate to fully embrace these objectives because they are not commonly mentioned at work. Once they see you are serious, they will begin to behave prosocially toward one another. The organization will be well on its way to healing and unlocking the productivity trapped within each of its producers.

You can ask people to trust one another, but trust is an outcome. Organizations move from trust to distrust in an instant and then very slowly move back toward trust once the source of the distrust is removed. From my experience, highly antisocial leaders have to be removed in order for the social system to heal. This idea is supported by neuroscientific research, as discussed in Chapter 6. The mere presence of antisocial individuals stimulates others' sympathetic nervous systems and has a debilitating impact on knowledge work. Getting socially corrosive and threatening people out of the social environment is critical so that deep trust can be reestablished. If you trust (and verify), you will receive trust in return.

By being completely transparent, reinforcing the need to care about one another by sharing and helping, and creating an organization where openness to others' ideas and thoughts is not just talk but reality, you will be well on your way to creating a trust-based culture. It takes time, but reinforcing these productivity-producing behaviors yields immediate dividends. Stopping socially corrosive behaviors always speeds execution and delivery, because it speeds collaboration.

There are other benefits to sharing. It is a great way to improve the level of knowledge in the organization. When people share what they know, they grow, as do the people they are teaching. Nothing increases your understanding more than explaining a concept or teaching someone else. Because your explanation has to be crisp, when you teach others, you have to go back and become intimately familiar with a subject area in order to clearly and fully explain it. Only when you have achieved deep and intimate understanding can you make it very clear to someone else.

We Learn . . .

    10% of what we read
    20% of what we hear
    30% of what we see
    50% of what we see and hear
    70% of what we discuss
    80% of what we experience
    95% of what we teach others

—William Glasser

Spend a lot of time thinking about your culture and observing the current state, so you can identity pockets of greatness as well as pockets of unhealthy sentiment and behavior. Be relentless, and don't tolerate passive resistance, because it destroys the return on human capital.

Institutional Experience

Great talent is not a commodity, and institutional experience is costly but indispensable. Build it, grow it, cultivate it—do whatever you have to do to ensure you have plenty. As I've reinforced elsewhere, institutional experience is acquired only on the job, inside your organization. Time to competency can take years because of the incredible complexity created by over 50 years of continuous investment in automation, so it is a key productivity driver.

Given its complexity, IT is a talent game if ever there was one. Deep institutional experience and aptitude combine together to create a true source of competitive advantage, especially in IT, where new solutions emerge every year, new software-based products and services are brought to market, and hyperspecialization is the norm. Over time, institutional experience becomes intimate understanding, competency grows, and the pace of knowledge work quickens while accuracy increases. The diverse productivity potential of highly experienced talent is conspicuous to leaders. Top performers have significantly more of what it takes to be effective: raw creativity, aptitude, knowledge, and a shorter time to competency, which leads to broader and deeper experience. Likewise, the productivity potential of teams varies greatly because IT is inherently social, requiring deep and meaningful collaboration to build anything. Organizations with the right blend of talent, deep experience, and accumulated social capital are both fast and brilliant.

Beyond a doubt, knowledge workers are *not* interchangeable parts. They never were. Aptitude should be sought after; institutional experience has high productive value and should be cultivated; the emotional drivers of knowledge worker productivity should be leveraged to stimulate higher levels of creativity and competitive advantage. But none of this value can be unlocked unless we see it, manage it, measure it, and use it.

IT Best Practices: In Context

IT best practices have been thoroughly documented in frameworks like Information Technology Infrastructure Library (ITIL) and Control Objectives for Information and Related Technology (COBIT), and there are many, many professional certifications. But none of these best practices work well unless they are a tightly coupled element in your overarching design. Figure 14.5 shows how best practices are intimately tied to your organizational design, governance, and culture. In summary, the organizational model defines how work is organized (covered earlier); IT best practices define how the work is done; governance defines how decisions are made; and culture energizes the whole structure. You can have an incredibly well-thought-out organizational model, but if you do not have the right practices and a clearly defined process for making decisions, then you can't run your department or division; if the culture isn't collaborative, open, and transparent, then none of these best practices work well. IT has to be approached in a holistic manner, and the approach ultimately has to have all the ingredients to create a highly effective division.

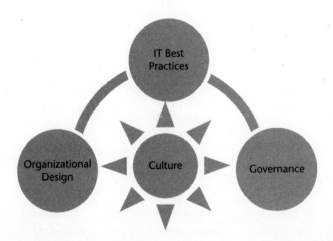

Figure 14.5   Best Practices in Context

There are many practices in IT, and you must prioritize how you address them using a combination of risk and business exigency to decide where to start. Normally I do this through governance. In a nutshell, governance defines how decisions are made, and by whom, and it is an important set of mechanisms that communicate a clear engagement model. In an organization, ambiguity about how to get something done greatly reduces productivity, as people use the informal social network to navigate to an answer; absent a clearly defined governance model that defines the committees and processes one must engage to gain approvals, acquire technology, and so on, IT becomes cumbersome and chaotic to work in; when multiple people think they own something, then turf wars begin, and relationships are damaged. A well-defined governance model helps create deeper collaboration and protects relationships, which enable more productivity to flow. Keep in mind that building a comprehensive, well-functioning governance model takes time, so manage expectations accordingly.

Figure 14.6 shows a governance model that you can use to begin configuring how IT will be governed in your organization.

Every governance area has a governance committee, a chairperson, a charter, and an improvement plan so that efficiency increases by removing as

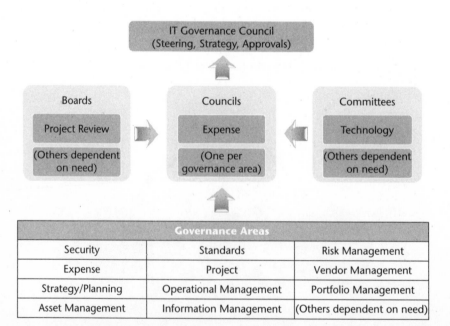

Figure 14.6 IT Governance Structure

much bureaucracy as possible. Make sure it is simple to engage each committee, and clear when a team has to present to it. Creating checklists that allow teams to bypass committees ensures that teams find the governance process efficient.

To build your governance, make a list of every process area for which governance is needed. You can refer to a number of reference frameworks to compile an initial inventory, but make sure the final list is based on your actual needs. Once you have the inventory, you need to establish the current state of maturity, by examining each governance mechanism to assess how well it is operating. For this, I recommend you use a *capability maturity* framework. Many different ones exist, but using a clear one, such as the Software Engineering Institute's Capability Maturity Model (CMM), will enable rapid adoption and assessment. The framework consists of six levels, beginning with nonexistent and moving through five levels of maturity ranging from initial to mature. Develop a scorecard of the different control areas, assessing and grading each by risk and maturity. You can use this model to set goals, measure progress, and communicate your maturity to your organization and senior management.

The IT governance committee oversees all governance, approves every policy recommendation, and ultimately owns IT policies. Governance within IT takes direction from any enterprise governance committees and aligns with policies issued by them. That said, there is a need for policies within IT, but I strongly recommend that *less is more*. Organizations with too many policies end up with areas out of compliance, lack of understanding, and difficulty matching policies to roles—the policy structure becomes unwieldy.

When looking at the human factors of IT, governance helps drive transparency, deepen collaboration, and strengthen relationships by leaving decisions to committees versus individuals; governance creates organizational trust, improves the sharing of information, drives inclusion versus exclusion by design, and gives people a voice. All of this is critical to the functioning of IT. My leadership team acted as the chairpersons on the committees, and their direct reports chaired any boards that reported to them. This method reinforced the importance of governance, and I supported the governance function with a small, dedicated team that focused on how it was aligned and the order in which the mechanisms were deployed. The IT governance council had overall ownership of the program, drove prioritization, and measured performance.

Best Practices in Detail

You will have to turn the following list of practices into running processes that engage every part of your organization, as functionally required. I included them so you can identify what gaps exist in your area, which will help you determine your phasing.

They are:

- Organizational design
- Cultural design
- Business-aligned technology strategy
- Portfolio planning and demand management
- Security
- Operational risk management
  - Disaster recovery
  - Critical infrastructure
- Data center strategy
- IT general controls
- Governance
- Change management
- Technology acquisition
- Contract management
- Vendor management
- System development life cycles
- Asset management
- Workforce planning
- Program and project management
- Expense management (18-month contract renewal pipeline)
- Application portfolio planning
- Finance and chargeback
- Service management (ITIL)
- Information management
- Communication strategy (downward and across IT and the business)
- Communication (upward to the board and management)
- Capacity management
- Architecture and engineering
- Operational performance management (operations oversight)
- Human resource processes (performance, succession, etc.)
- Computer operations (your run processes)

Win over the Hearts and Minds of the Business

IT is a service bureau that must be as tightly woven into the fabric of the business as possible. Don't create artificial boundaries, as if IT is a distinct entity. Yes, the tools are different, and it is a profession, but we automate business products and services, so we are an integral part of *the business*. Don't ever lose sight of this. Also don't lose sight of your role as a cost center, not a profit center. Some people are more equal than others, and in business, IT is a servant, not a master. For that reason, I found it useful to *lead from behind*. Although you have a seat at the table, it was always clear to me that I was a custodian of the business's money and therefore treated it with respect, being careful to optimize expenses and deliver a lot of value.

To become a reliable business partner, put a collaborative organization in place, build strong practices within a productive social climate, and be candid. The business will see and feel the difference. Results do speak for themselves, and they speak loudly. Keep execution crisp, be open and honest about the organization's capabilities, build strong relationships, drive high levels of social cohesion across business and IT, make sure the challenges are known, and engage the business as you fix them.

Conclusion

The message I want to close with is that sometimes extremely complex challenges can be managed by focusing on foundational elements. By putting what you have read in place, you will be able to turn a sluggish, overweight, and unreliable organization into an efficient, optimized, and proficient producer. You'll exceed your expense objectives, optimize project execution, deliver a reliable, well-engineered infrastructure, create transparent decision making, and unleash innovation by unlocking your talent's potential.

With the right organizational structure and a healthy, collaborative working environment, information and ideas will flow between the business and IT and within IT. Productivity will increase with each project as highly competent professionals build the deep and valuable experience that comes only with time on the job. Each project is an investment not only in products and services but in building and growing talent. Embrace the human infrastructure and watch productivity grow.

You unleash talent and drive productivity by building trust, which strengthens social cohesion, leading to deep and meaningful collaboration and real business results. Care deeply about your people, and they will care about the company in return. In an environment where people count, it is easier to build success than would otherwise be possible. My results across companies were always excellent, because the human factors of IT infused every design decision that had to be made. The time to embrace your people is now. They aren't interchangeable parts—they never were.

Good luck on your journey.

ABOUT THE AUTHOR

Frank Wander is a former Fortune 250 chief information officer (CIO) and founder of the IT Excellence Institute, a social enterprise dedicated to the notion that IT can be a high-performing, flourishing part of any corporation. After spending many years transforming failed or failing IT divisions, Frank realized that the root cause of failure was cultures where socially corrosive and antisocial behaviors were prevalent. To turn these organizations around, he nurtured the human factors of productivity (trust, caring, collaboration, transparency, meaning, etc.) and blended these with IT best practices, creating a potent recipe for success.

Prior to starting the institute, Frank was the CIO at Guardian Life Insurance Company of America for more than five years, transforming the culture and capability of IT to deliver business projects on time and on budget across 90 percent of its portfolio. Before joining Guardian, Frank was the CIO for the Harry Fox Agency, where he led the company's IT team in the turnaround of a failed technology transformation initiative. Frank also served as CIO of Prudential Institutional, was president of an Internet start-up, and spent many years at Merrill Lynch in leadership roles spanning both IT and client services.

Frank is a regular speaker at conferences, and is frequently interviewed for articles. He is currently working on his second book, a video series on the human factors of productivity, and launching a seminar series designed to help companies understand that IT failure can be a relic of the past.

INDEX